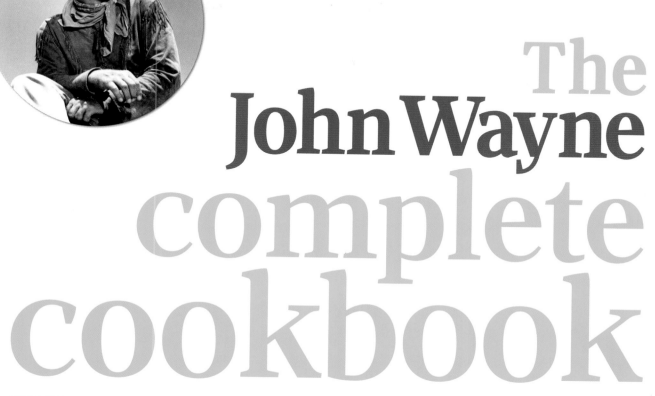

The John Wayne complete cookbook

THE ULTIMATE COLLECTION OF HOMESTYLE RECIPES FROM DUKE'S KITCHEN TO YOURS

MY FATHER WOULD HAVE EATEN STEAK AND POTATOES

at every meal, and the phrase "charred medium" still rings in my ears. As much as he enjoyed a well-prepared piece of meat, what John Wayne loved best about a meal was how it brought us all together. Gathered around the table, trading stories and laughs, a dinner at the end of a long day of work meant good times and better company. I'm pleased to share with you this collection of recipes and techniques, as well as some Wayne family secrets for how to get the most out of a bite to eat. Whether you're a tenderfoot in the kitchen or an old hand, there's something here for everyone—delivered with Duke's trademark no-nonsense style.

Dig in.

—ETHAN WAYNE

TABLE OF CONTENTS

FIRING UP A FEAST

John Wayne's character Capt. Jake Cutter makes a meal over an open fire as Stuart Whitman's Paul Regret looks on in *The Comancheros* (1961). Next time you take a trip to the great outdoors, bring along a camping skillet for chow time.

GRILLING BASICS

A LOT OF RECIPES IN THIS BOOK CALL FOR A GRILL. IT'S A SIMPLE CONCEPT: FIRE PLUS MEAT EQUALS DINNER. BUT IT CAN BE HARROWING TO THE UNINITIATED. KNOW WHAT YER DOIN' BEFORE FIRIN' IT UP, PILGRIM.

Lighting Your Grill

First, remove all ash and grease from your grill. A brush with metal bristles will scrape up all the charred fat and remove last month's flavors from your grill. If you don't have a grill brush, don't fret. You can use aluminum foil by crumpling it into a ball and handling it between your tongs. Next, crumple up several pieces of newspaper, place in the center of the grill and drizzle each with canola, vegetable or olive oil. Place a layer of small, dry sticks over the paper for kindling. Add a few pieces of charcoal near the center of the pile, then light the paper in several places. After the charcoal you've placed catches the flame and continues burning, use tongs to slowly add more charcoal until you have two full, even layers of briquettes. Once you've got your layers, stack them into a cone shape in the middle of your grill. In stormy or windy weather, you'll want to use a few more briquettes so your grill stays nice and hot.

Keeping Your Grill Perfect

Perfect, for grilling purposes, means hot, clean and lubricated. This will minimize outside flavors imparted by the grill and maximize the quality of your meal. In addition to preheating and cleaning your grill as just described, using a paper towel covered in oil can go a long way toward keeping your grill slick and minimizing the sticky, charred remains that tend to linger after you've served up the grub. Simply place the paper towel in your tongs and rub the grill with oil before you start cooking.

Direct or Indirect Heat

Before you start cooking, you'll have to make a decision between direct and indirect heat. Foods that take less than 30 minutes to cook over flame are best cooked directly. These include boneless chicken, steaks, fish fillets, hamburgers and hot dogs. All you really have to do is toss them on the grill and try not to torch them. Foods that take longer than 30 minutes are best grilled with indirect heat. Whole turkeys, bone-in chicken, brisket and other larger fare should be placed above a drip pan to create an effect similar to oven-roasting. If you're using charcoal, arrange your briquettes on the lower level against the drip pan before placing your meat on the grill. You can add water to the drip pan to provide some extra moisture, or get a little creative if you like and add something like apple juice for a bit of flavor.

No Thermometers

Sure, you could use a fancy probe thermometer to ensure you've got the temperature just right. But you can also use the thermometer God gave you: your hands. If you're cooking 1-inch slices of steak, rare meat will take about 15 to 20 minutes over a 350-degree grill—if you can only stand to hold your hand over the coals for around 7 seconds, it's cooking at 350 degrees F. At this temperature, a steak cooked to medium will be done in less than 25 minutes and a well-done one can take up to 30. To check the temperature of the meat, hold your hand down flat and push your thumb into the fleshiest part of the palm (see chart above). The softness of that spot will mimic the feel of a rare steak. Next, touch your thumb to the pads of each of your other fingers. By moving from the index finger to the pinky, you can compare the feel to that of a medium-rare, medium, medium-well and well-done steaks. And remember: You can always toss a steak back on the grill to bring it to a higher temperature—but you can't un-cook charbroiled meat.

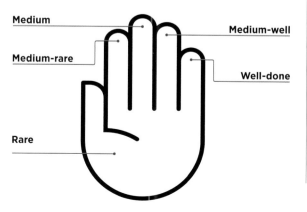

Medium · Medium-well · Medium-rare · Well-done · Rare

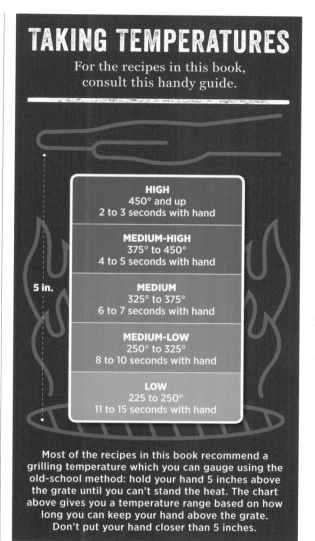

TAKING TEMPERATURES

For the recipes in this book, consult this handy guide.

5 in.

HIGH
450° and up
2 to 3 seconds with hand

MEDIUM-HIGH
375° to 450°
4 to 5 seconds with hand

MEDIUM
325° to 375°
6 to 7 seconds with hand

MEDIUM-LOW
250° to 325°
8 to 10 seconds with hand

LOW
225 to 250°
11 to 15 seconds with hand

Most of the recipes in this book recommend a grilling temperature which you can gauge using the old-school method: hold your hand 5 inches above the grate until you can't stand the heat. The chart above gives you a temperature range based on how long you can keep your hand above the grate. Don't put your hand closer than 5 inches.

Putting Out the Fire

After covering your grill, close the vents and allow your coals to burn out. Then let the ashes cool for at least 48 hours and dispose of them in a container that isn't flammable. If you absolutely have to cut that 48 hours short, remove each brick individually with long tongs and submerge them either in water or sand.

CAST IRON 101

HOW TO SEASON AND CLEAN YOUR CAST IRON

Seasoning Your Pan

Without a good layer of seasoning, a cast-iron pan will eventually start to corrode and rust. Though the initial seasoning (or re-seasoning) can be a lengthy process, your hard work will be well worth it—a properly seasoned pan can be passed down for generations!

If your cast-iron pan is brand new (even if it claims to be pre-seasoned), or getting dull or rusted, it's time to season it.

You'll Need

Dish soap
Sponge or stiff brush
Paper towels
Vegetable oil or shortening

Directions

1. Preheat your oven to 325 degrees F.

2. Wash your skillet with hot, soapy water, scrubbing hard to remove any rust. Usually you should not use soap to clean your cast iron, but it's OK to do this prior to seasoning.

3. Dry your cast-iron pan and wipe it out with paper towels. If any grit comes off on the towels, rewash your pan.

4. Using another paper towel, apply a thin layer of oil or shortening to the inside and outside of your skillet.

5. Place the skillet upside down on your oven's center rack, with a sheet pan or aluminum foil on a rack below it to catch any drips.

6. Bake the pan for 1 hour. Turn off the oven and let the pan cool completely before removing it.

Cleaning Your Pan

1. Clean your pan right away, while it's still hot or warm—this is especially important if you've cooked something acidic, like tomatoes. Do not leave it in the sink or let it soak in water, as this may cause rust.

2. Do not use soap, steel wool or a dishwasher to clean your pan. Using a stiff brush or the rough side of a sponge, scrub your pan well and rinse with hot water. Repeat as necessary.

3. To remove extra-stubborn food residue, scrub with salt or boil water in the pan to loosen the food.

4. Once clean, dry your pan on the stove over low heat.

5. While still warm, apply a very light layer of oil on the pan with a paper towel, and then buff to remove any excess oil.

6. Store the skillet in a dry place.

BIG JAKE'S BIG BREAKFAST SKILLET
PAGE 23

BREAKFAST

Start your day off on the right boot with these mouth-watering meals that will keep you sated all day.

Maple Pancakes

Ringo Kid's Bacon Pancakes

Classic Scratch Biscuits

Davy Crockett's Breakfast Casserole

Sean Thornton's Corned Beef Hash Frittata

Big Jake's Big Breakfast Skillet

French Toast Casserole

Ham and Egg Skillet Strata

Home (on the Range) Fries

Huevos Rancheros

MAPLE PANCAKES

These pancakes will have your family flipping out over flapjacks in a whole new way.

PROVISIONS

- 12 slices thick-cut bacon
- ¾ cup plus 2 Tbsp. oats
- ¾ cup flour
- ½ cup cornstarch
- 1½ tsp. baking powder
- ½ tsp. baking soda
- ½ tsp. kosher salt
- 1 cup buttermilk
- 2 large eggs
- ¼ cup maple syrup
- 2 Tbsp. bacon grease

PREP

1. Preheat oven to 200 degrees F.

2. Cut the bacon in half lengthwise, and then cut into ½-inch pieces. Put in a large, cold skillet and turn the heat to medium. Cook the bacon, stirring frequently, until browned and crispy, about 10 minutes. Remove the bacon pieces from the grease with a slotted spoon and drain on paper towels. Reserve 1 Tbsp. of bacon grease for the batter and a little for greasing the pancake griddle.

3. Put the oats in a blender or food processor and grind to a powder. Add the flour, cornstarch, baking powder and soda, salt, buttermilk, eggs, maple syrup and 1 Tbsp. reserved bacon grease. Blend until combined, scraping down the sides of the blender or food processor once or twice. Let batter sit for 10 minutes to thicken slightly. Reserve a small handful of the bacon pieces for garnish and fold the rest into the batter.

4. Heat a griddle or large skillet over medium-low. Brush with some reserved bacon grease and pour or ladle about ¼ cup of batter out for each pancake. Cook until the edges of the pancake start to look dry and there are some holes in the top of the pancakes, about 1 ½ minutes. Flip and cook until the bottoms are browned and the pancakes feel firm to the touch, about another minute. Put pancakes on a plate and keep warm in the oven while cooking remaining batter.

John Wayne, Dolores del Rio and John Ford on the set of *The Searchers* (1956).

RINGO KID'S BACON PANCAKES

These sweet and savory treats are so good,
they should be outlawed.

PROVISIONS

10	slices bacon
4	Tbsp. bacon grease
1½	cups all-purpose flour
1½	cups cornmeal
½	tsp. kosher salt
1	Tbsp. baking powder
1½	tsp. baking soda
2	large eggs
3	Tbsp. maple syrup, plus more for serving
1	Tbsp. pure vanilla extract
2-2½	cups buttermilk
	Butter, for cooking the pancakes

PREP

1. Preheat the oven to 200 degrees F.

2. Cut the bacon in small pieces. Place in a large skillet and cook over medium heat, stirring occasionally, until very crispy, 12 to 15 minutes. Remove the bacon with a slotted spoon and drain the bacon on paper towels. Reserve 4 Tbsp. of bacon grease, more if you want to cook the pancakes in bacon grease instead of butter.

3. In a large mixing bowl, whisk together the flour, cornmeal, salt, baking powder and baking soda.

4. In a separate bowl, whisk together the eggs, 3 Tbsp. maple syrup, vanilla and 2 cups buttermilk. Add the wet ingredients to the dry ingredients and stir to combine. Stir in the reserved bacon grease. If the batter is too thick, add a little more buttermilk. Stir in half of the cooked bacon.

5. Heat a skillet over medium-low until hot. Melt about 1 Tbsp. of butter on the skillet and ladle ¼ cup of batter per pancake. Cook until the edges of the pancake start to look dry and the bottom is golden brown, about 3 minutes. Flip and cook another 2 to 3 minutes or until golden brown. Put on a heatproof plate and keep warm in the oven while cooking the rest of the pancakes.

6. Serve the pancakes with maple syrup and the rest of the bacon on top.

George Bancroft, John Wayne, Andy Devine and Francis Ford, in *Stagecoach* (1939).

CLASSIC SCRATCH BISCUITS

The recipe for these homestyle country biscuits is a lot like a family heirloom: something to treasure, then pass on.

PROVISIONS

- 1½ cups flour, plus more for rolling
- ¾ cup cornstarch
- 1 Tbsp. baking powder
- 1 tsp. kosher or fine sea salt
- 6 Tbsp. butter, cut into small pieces
- ¾ cup milk

John Wayne and his son Ethan on the *Wild Goose*.

PREP

1. Preheat oven to 400 degrees F. Line a baking sheet with parchment paper or a silicone baking mat.

2. Whisk together the flour, starch, baking powder and salt. Cut the butter into the flour either with a pastry cutter, two knives or by rubbing the butter into the flour with your fingers. Make sure you leave some larger pieces of butter. Add the liquid, starting with ½ cup and gradually adding a little more at a time, mixing until the dough comes together.

3. Put a little flour on a work surface and dump out the dough. Knead 3 or 4 times then either roll or pat it out to about ½-inch thick. Cut into biscuits using a 2 ½-inch cookie cutter. You can gently reform the dough to cut more biscuits.

4. Place the biscuits on the prepared baking sheet and bake for 20 minutes or until lightly browned. Serve warm.

WAYNE FAMILY TIP

Make sure your butter is cold at the start to achieve maximum flakiness.

DAVY CROCKETT'S BREAKFAST CASSEROLE

Start your day with this hearty meal and you'll have enough energy to defend the Alamo (or anything else).

PROVISIONS

- 6 bacon slices, diced
- 1 cup diced green peppers
- 1 cup diced yellow onion
- 3 cups peeled and diced sweet potatoes
- 1 tsp. salt
- 1 tsp. garlic powder
- 1 tsp. onion powder
- 1 lb. breakfast sausage
- 1 (9-oz.) package fresh spinach
- 12 large eggs

PREP

1. Preheat oven to 350 degrees F.

2. In a saucepan over medium heat, cook the bacon until it renders a good amount of fat. Add the peppers, onion, sweet potatoes, salt, garlic powder and onion powder.

3. Cook for 5 minutes, stirring continuously. Add the breakfast sausage. Crumble it up as it cooks for 2 to 3 minutes. Add the spinach and stir until wilted. (Covering the saucepan will speed this up.)

4. Transfer the mixture to a 9- by 13-inch casserole dish, spreading it evenly and pressing down.

5. Crack the eggs on top. Bake until the egg whites are set and yolks are done to your liking, 5 to 10 minutes for slightly runny yolks or longer for firmer yolks.

Hank Worden, Frankie Avalon, John Wayne and Chill Wills in *The Alamo* (1960).

SEAN THORNTON'S CORNED BEEF HASH FRITTATA

One taste of this hearty breakfast, and your taste buds will be dancing a jig.

PROVISIONS

- 1 lb. small red potatoes, scrubbed, unpeeled and cut into ½-in. dice
- 1½ tsp. kosher or fine sea salt
- ¾ tsp. pepper
- 10 large eggs
- 3 Tbsp. heavy cream
- 1 Tbsp. spicy brown mustard
- 1 Tbsp. vegetable oil
- 1 medium white or yellow onion, diced
- ½ lb. deli corned beef, diced
- 2 Tbsp. chopped chives

PREP

1. Place the potatoes in a microwave-safe bowl with the salt and pepper and stir. Cover the bowl with plastic wrap and microwave on high power for 6 minutes or until tender.

2. Preheat the oven to 400 degrees F.

3. Whisk together the eggs, cream and mustard.

4. Heat oil in a cast-iron skillet over medium until it begins to shimmer. Add onion and cook until tender and translucent, about 5 minutes. Add the potatoes and corned beef. Pour egg mixture over top and use a spatula to make sure eggs surround the potatoes and corned beef. Cook for 1 minute on the stove then transfer the pan to oven. Cook for 12–14 minutes or until the eggs are fully set. Top with chives.

John Wayne, Ward Bond and Victor McLaglen in *The Quiet Man* (1952).

DID YOU KNOW?

Maureen O'Hara testified in front of Congress in 1979 in support of Duke receiving a Congressional Gold Medal.

BIG JAKE'S BIG BREAKFAST SKILLET

This breakfast brings smiles to the faces of the whole family. Guaranteed.

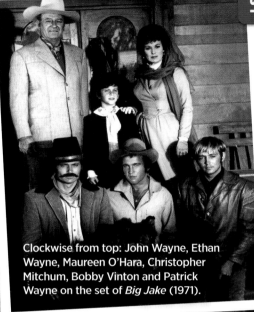

Clockwise from top: John Wayne, Ethan Wayne, Maureen O'Hara, Christopher Mitchum, Bobby Vinton and Patrick Wayne on the set of *Big Jake* (1971).

PROVISIONS

- 6 slices bacon
- 4 cups grated potatoes (from 2–3 large russet potatoes)
- 1 medium white or yellow onion, grated
-   Kosher or fine sea salt, to taste
-   Pepper, to taste
- 6 large eggs
- 2 cups grated cheddar cheese, divided
- 4 green onions, sliced

PREP

1. Preheat oven to 350 degrees F.

2. Place the bacon in a cold, large cast-iron skillet. Turn heat to medium and cook on the stovetop until the bacon is crispy, turning often. Remove the bacon and drain on paper towels. Add the potatoes and onions to the hot bacon grease, add a large pinch of both salt and pepper and stir several times to mix well. Raise the heat to medium-high and cook until the potatoes start to brown on the bottom, about 6 minutes.

3. Whisk the eggs in a mixing bowl, add 1 cup of the cheese and a large pinch of salt and pepper, and stir to combine. Pour the egg mixture over the potatoes, sprinkle the remaining cheese on top, crumble the bacon on top, add the green onions and bake for 10 minutes or until the eggs are set.

WAYNE FAMILY TIP

To cook your bacon perfectly, add a little bit of water to the pan. It helps cut down on the possibility of burnt bacon.

FAMILY DINING TIME
Duke sits with his children Ethan, Marisa and Aissa and his wife Pilar, c. 1969. Pilar co-wrote a 1987 memoir about her marriage to the legend titled *John Wayne: My Life with the Duke*.

FRENCH TOAST CASSEROLE

Might as well unbuckle your belt
before tucking into this breakfast, pilgrim.
You'll need the extra room.

PROVISIONS

6 large eggs

2½ cups milk

¼ cup maple syrup,
plus more to serve

1 tsp. vanilla extract

1 tsp. ground cinnamon

½ tsp. salt

12 slices sandwich bread

4 Tbsp. butter, melted

PREP

1. In a large mixing bowl, whisk together
the eggs, milk, ¼ cup maple syrup, vanilla
extract, cinnamon and salt. Cut the bread
into 1-in. cubes. Add the bread to the egg/
milk mixture. Stir gently to combine. Let sit
for 30 minutes, stirring gently occasionally.

2. Preheat oven to 375 degrees F.

3. Pour the bread mixture into a cast-
iron skillet and gently press down with a
spatula. Top with the melted butter and
bake for 55 minutes or until golden brown
and set. Let cool for 5 minutes before
serving. Serve with extra maple syrup.

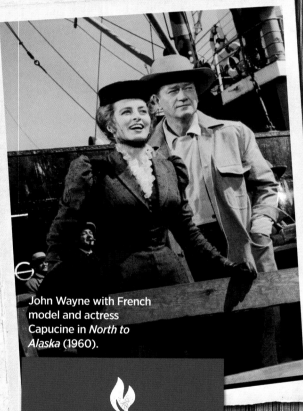

John Wayne with French
model and actress
Capucine in *North to
Alaska* (1960).

WAYNE FAMILY TIP

Use real maple syrup instead
of pancake syrup. Not only
does it taste better, but there
are also no artificial or added
ingredients.

HAM AND EGG SKILLET STRATA

Start the day off right by whipping together this tasty and filling breakfast—there's enough for the whole family!

PROVISIONS

- 1 Tbsp. vegetable oil
- 1 Tbsp. butter
- 6 slices sandwich bread, cut into pieces
- ½ lb. thick sliced deli ham, diced
- 4 green onions, sliced
- 6 large eggs
- 1½ cups milk
- 1 cup grated cheddar cheese
- 1 Tbsp. Worcestershire sauce
- ½ tsp. salt
- ½ tsp. dry mustard
- ½ tsp. pepper

PREP

1. Preheat oven to 425 degrees F.

2. Heat a cast-iron skillet over medium heat for 2 minutes. Add the oil and butter. As soon as the butter is melted, add the bread cubes. Toss to coat and cook, stirring occasionally, until the bread is slightly toasted, about 5 minutes. Add the ham and green onions and cook, stirring, for another minute.

3. In a large mixing bowl, whisk together the eggs, milk, cheese, Worcestershire sauce, salt, mustard and pepper. Pour the egg mixture over the bread and press down gently with a spatula.

4. Bake for 20 minutes, or until golden brown and set. Let cool 5 minutes before serving.

John Wayne and Gail Russell in a scene from *Angel and the Badman* (1947).

HOME (ON THE RANGE) FRIES

The smell of these potatoes frying in the pan will get 'em out of bed in a hurry.

PROVISIONS

- **2 lb. red potatoes,** scrubbed and unpeeled, cut into ¾-in. dice
- **5 Tbsp. vegetable oil,** divided
- **1½ tsp. kosher or fine sea salt**
- **1 tsp. pepper**
- **1 medium white or yellow onion,** diced
- **1 red bell pepper,** seeded, deveined and diced
- **2 garlic cloves,** minced

PREP

1. Place the potatoes, 1 Tbsp. oil, salt and pepper in a microwave-safe bowl. Cover with plastic wrap and microwave on high power for 7 to 10 minutes or until tender. Drain well.

2. Heat 2 Tbsp. of oil in a cast-iron skillet over medium until the oil starts to shimmer. Add the onion and red bell pepper and cook, stirring occasionally, until tender and starting to brown. Add the garlic and cook for 30 seconds, stirring. Transfer the mixture to the bowl with the potatoes and mix well.

3. Add the remaining 2 Tbsp. of oil to the now empty skillet and heat until shimmering. Add the potato mixture and flatten it gently with a spatula. Cook, undisturbed, for 5 to 7 minutes or until browned on the bottom.

4. Flip the potatoes, one portion at a time, with a spatula and gently flatten down. Continue to cook, flipping the potatoes every 2 to 3 minutes, until well browned, about 15 minutes. Season to taste with more salt and pepper.

John Wayne in *Lawless Range* (1935).

HUEVOS RANCHEROS

Treat yourself to this Southwestern recipe that's almost as classic as Duke himself.

PROVISIONS

- 1 Tbsp. vegetable oil
- 1 small white or yellow onion, diced
- 1 (14.5-oz.) can diced fire roasted tomatoes, undrained
- 1 Tbsp. tomato paste
- 1 (15-oz.) can kidney or pinto beans, rinsed and drained
- 1 (4-oz.) can chopped mild green chilies, drained
- 1 tsp. dried cumin
- ½ tsp. chipotle pepper
- 1 tsp. kosher or fine sea salt, plus more to taste
- ½ tsp. pepper, plus more to taste
- 4 corn tortillas
- 2 Tbsp. butter
- 4 large eggs
- 1 avocado, sliced, to serve
- 2 Tbsp. minced fresh cilantro, to serve

John Wayne and Rock Hudson in *The Undefeated* (1969).

PREP

1. Heat oil in a cast-iron skillet over medium-high until it shimmers. Add the onion and cook until tender and translucent, about 4 minutes. Add the tomatoes with the juice and cook for about 1 minute, stirring. Add the tomato paste and cook, stirring for another minute. Add the beans, chilies, cumin, chipotle pepper, 1 tsp. salt and ½ tsp. pepper. Let simmer, uncovered, for about 10 minutes, or until slightly thickened. Keep warm until serving.

2. Heat another cast-iron skillet over medium-high. When hot, add the tortillas, one at a time, and cook until they soften and start to brown in some spots. Remove from skillet and keep warm. Repeat until all tortillas are cooked.

3. Reduce the heat to medium, add the butter and let it melt. Crack the eggs into the skillet, season with salt and pepper and cook 2 to 3 minutes or until desired degree of doneness.

4. To serve, place some of the tomato sauce on a plate, top with an egg, avocado slices and cilantro and serve with the warm tortillas.

PERFECT PORTERHOUSE
PAGE 74

STEAK

Classic and straightforward, steak was Duke's favorite, and these recipes exemplify everything he loved about it.

RINGO KID'S SKIRT STEAK

Take your tastebuds on a wild ride with this hearty dish.

PROVISIONS

- 4 Tbsp. brown sugar
- 2 Tbsp. kosher salt
- 2 Tbsp. smoked paprika
- 1 Tbsp. garlic powder
- 2 tsp. cayenne pepper
- 2½ lb. skirt steak
- Vegetable oil, for grill

PREP

1. In a small mixing bowl, combine the brown sugar, salt, paprika, garlic powder and cayenne pepper. Press the mixture generously on both sides of the skirt steak. Let sit at room temperature while preparing the grill.

2. Prepare grill for direct heat. Brush the grill grates with oil.

3. Pat the steak dry and grill for 2 to 3 minutes per side for medium rare. Cover the steak with foil and let rest for 10 minutes before slicing.

Claire Trevor and John Wayne in *Stagecoach* (1939).

DID YOU KNOW?

Duke's popularity remains unmatched more than 40 years after his death. He is the only deceased actor to consistently place in the Harris Poll's list of Top 10 favorite actors.

BRANNIGAN'S LONDON BROIL

Detective Brannigan was relentless in his pursuit of justice. Once your guests taste this London broil, they'll be relentless in their pursuit of the recipe.

PROVISIONS

- 1 (2- to 2½-lb.) London broil
  Vegetable oil, for grill

BLUE CHEESE SAUCE

- ⅔ cup sour cream
- ⅓ cup mayonnaise
- 2 tsp. Worcestershire sauce
- 4 oz. crumbled blue cheese
  Kosher or fine sea salt and pepper, to taste

MARINADE

- ½ cup olive oil
- ¼ cup soy sauce
- ¼ cup red wine vinegar
- 1 Tbsp. Dijon mustard
- 1 Tbsp. Worcestershire sauce
- 2 garlic cloves, minced

PREP

BLUE CHEESE SAUCE

1. Combine all ingredients in a mixing bowl. Season to taste with salt and pepper. Cover with plastic wrap and refrigerate until ready to serve.

MARINADE

1. Whisk all ingredients together in a mixing bowl. Pour the marinade into a plastic food storage bag. Place the London broil in the bag, flipping several times to coat the meat with the marinade. Let sit at room temperature for 30 minutes or refrigerate for up to 24 hours. If marinating in the refrigerator, let sit at room temperature for 20 to 30 minutes before grilling.

STEAK

1. Prepare the grill for direct heat and preheat to medium-high.

2. Remove the meat from the marinade, discarding the marinade and pat dry with paper towels.

3. Brush the grates of the grill with oil and grill the meat 6 to 8 minutes per side, with the lid open, or until it reaches an internal temperature of 125 degrees F for medium-rare. Place the meat on a cutting board, cover with foil and let rest for 10 minutes before serving. Slice thinly across the grain and serve with the blue cheese sauce.

Duke on the set of *Brannigan* (1975).

DID YOU KNOW?

While many of his characters fearlessly wielded firearms to fend off wrongdoers, John Wayne only portrayed a modern, big city police officer in 1974's *McQ* and 1975's *Brannigan*.

RED RIVER RIB EYE

You don't have to survive a long, treacherous cattle drive to deserve this juicy cut.

PROVISIONS

Vegetable oil, for grill

4 (10-oz.) boneless rib eye steaks, 1-in. thick

COFFEE RUB

2 Tbsp. finely ground coffee

2 Tbsp. chili powder

1 Tbsp. light or dark brown sugar

1½ tsp. pepper

1 tsp. kosher or fine sea salt

PREP

1. Combine all the rub ingredients together in a small bowl.

2. Remove steaks from the refrigerator, brush all sides with oil. Rub and press the rub into all sides of the steaks. Let sit at room temperature for 20 to 30 minutes.

3. Prepare grill for direct heat and preheat to high. Brush the grates with oil.

4. Grill steaks 4 to 6 minutes per side or until they reach an internal temperature of 125 degrees F for medium rare.

5. Let steaks rest for 5 to 10 minutes before serving.

John Wayne in *Red River* (1948).

WAYNE FAMILY TIP

When steak is on a skewer, it cooks faster than when grilled as a whole cut. You'll want to stand by the grill and keep an eye on these skewers as overcooking can ruin a steak. Aim for medium or medium-rare.

SIZZLIN' STEAK SKEWERS

The best part about eating your steak on a skewer?
It frees up a hand to hold a cold beverage, just like you deserve.

PROVISIONS

24–26 wooden skewers

2 lb. skirt steak

MARINADE

⅓ cup olive oil

2 Tbsp. lime juice

1 tsp. ground cumin

½ tsp. kosher or fine sea salt

¼ tsp. pepper

PESTO

2 garlic cloves, roughly chopped

1 jalapeño pepper, seeded, deveined and chopped

¼ cup pine nuts

4 cups fresh cilantro

4 Tbsp. lime juice (from 2 limes)

1 Tbsp. agave or honey

1 tsp. kosher or fine sea salt

½ tsp. pepper

6 Tbsp. olive oil

Vegetable oil, for grill

PREP

1. Soak the skewers in water for 30 to 45 minutes.

2. Cut the steak into 8-in. lengths. Lay on a plate or baking sheet in a single layer and place in the freezer for 30 to 45 minutes to make slicing easier. Remove from freezer and slice lengthwise into ¼-in. pieces. Let sit at room temperature while making the marinade.

MARINADE

1. Whisk all the marinade ingredients together in a small mixing bowl. Pour into a large freezer bag, add the sliced steak and toss a few times to coat. Let rest at room temperature for 20 to 30 minutes.

PESTO

1. Place the garlic, jalapeño, and pine nuts in a food processor. Process until everything is finely ground. Add the cilantro, lime juice, agave, salt and pepper. Process until fully combined. Add the olive oil and process until nearly smooth. Place in a serving bowl.

STEAK

1. Prepare the grill for direct heat and preheat to high.

2. Remove the steak from the marinade. Discard the marinade and thread the steak onto the pre-soaked skewers.

3. Brush grill grates with oil. Grill the skewers 1 to 2 minutes per side keeping the lid to the grill open. Serve with the pesto.

Duke in *The Sons of Katie Elder* (1965).

TEXAS TACOS

These skirt steak tacos are just like the Lone Star state—big and full of flavor.

John Wayne, Richard Widmark and Laurence Harvey in *The Alamo* (1960).

PROVISIONS

SALSA

- 2   jalapeños
- 6   plum tomatoes, cut in half lengthwise
- 1   small red onion, sliced ¼-inch thick
- 4   Tbsp. lime juice
- ½   tsp. kosher or fine sea salt
- ½   cup cilantro leaves
-     Vegetable oil, for tomatoes

TACOS

- 12 corn tortillas
-     Vegetable oil, for grill
- 1½ lb. flank or skirt steak
-     Kosher or fine sea salt, to taste
-     Pepper, to taste
- ½   small red or white onion, finely diced
- ½   cup cilantro leaves, finely chopped

PREP

SALSA

1. Prepare grill for direct heat and preheat to high.

2. Place the jalapeños directly on the grill. Cook with lid down, turning occasionally, until the skin is charred all over, about 10 to 12 minutes.

Take off the grill, place in a small bowl and cover with plastic wrap. Let rest at least 5 minutes.

3. Brush the cut sides of the tomatoes with oil and place directly on the grill. Brush both sides of the onion with oil and place directly on the grill. Grill with the lid closed until the tomatoes are a little charred and starting to soften, about 10 minutes. Grill the onions, flipping once, until charred and beginning to soften. Keep the grill lit.

4. Rub the jalapeños to remove the charred skin. For a mild salsa, cut in half and scrape out the seeds. Place in a blender or food processor with the grilled tomatoes and onions. Add the lime juice and blend until smooth, scraping down the sides of container as needed. Add the cilantro and pulse several times, you want to still see flecks of the cilantro. Place in a serving bowl.

TACOS

1. Wrap the tortillas in foil and place on the top rack of the grill or on the coolest side to warm them.

2. Brush the grill grates with oil.

3. Season the steak with salt and pepper and grill with the lid open for 2 minutes per side. Let sit 5 minutes before serving. Cut the steak into thin slices.

4. Serve the meat in the tortillas with the onion and cilantro and the salsa on the side.

DID YOU KNOW?

The Lubbock Christian University Library in Texas features a 13-ton boulder carved to resemble John Wayne's face. The boulder was carved by Brett-Livingstone Strong in 1979.

NO-FUSS FILET MIGNON

Enjoy the taste of one of the most tender cuts of meat around without any bit of hassle.

PROVISIONS

CHIVE BUTTER

- 6 Tbsp. butter, at room temperature
- 2 Tbsp. minced chives

STEAK

- 4 filet mignon steaks, 1½-in. thick, about 6 oz. each
- Olive oil, for steak
- Kosher or fine sea salt, to taste
- Pepper, to taste
- Vegetable oil, for grill

PREP

CHIVE BUTTER

1. In a small mixing bowl, mash the butter with a fork. Add the chives and mix well. Place a piece of plastic wrap on a flat work surface, and scoop the butter on to the plastic wrap. Roll into a cylinder and twist the ends of plastic wrap. Refrigerate at least 30 minutes. Can be made a week in advance and stored in the refrigerator.

STEAK

1. Remove the steaks from the refrigerator half an hour before you plan to grill them. Drizzle with olive oil on all sides and season generously with salt and pepper. Let sit at room temperature for about 30 minutes.

2. Prepare grill for direct heat and preheat to medium-high. Brush the grates with oil. Grill the steaks with the lid closed for 3 to 5 minutes per side (internal temperature of between 125–130 degrees F) for medium rare.

3. Let steaks rest for 5 minutes. Cut the butter into 4 slices and place one slice on each steak. Serve immediately.

John Wayne in *Flame of Barbary Coast* (1945).

FREEDOM FAJITAS

Any flag-waving patriot knows American cuisine is made great by influences from around the globe, and these fajitas are evidence of that.

PROVISIONS

MARINADE

- ¾ cup olive oil
- ½ cup orange juice
- ¼ cup lime juice
- 1 jalapeño, minced
- 2 garlic cloves, minced
- 1 tsp. ground cumin
- 1 tsp. dried oregano
- 1 tsp. kosher or fine sea salt
- ½ tsp. pepper

FAJITAS

- 2 lb. skirt steak
- 1 large onion, thinly sliced
- 1 green bell pepper, seeded, deveined and thinly sliced
- 1 red bell pepper, seeded, deveined and thinly sliced
- 1 yellow or orange bell pepper, seeded, deveined and thinly sliced
- 1 Tbsp. vegetable oil, plus more to prepare grill
- Salt and pepper, to taste
- 12 flour tortillas or 24 corn tortillas, warmed

FOR SERVING, OPTIONAL

- Salsa
- Sour cream
- Avocado slices
- Guacamole
- Grated cheese

PREP

1. Combine all the marinade ingredients in a mixing bowl and whisk well.

2. Place the steak in a large food storage bag, pour in half the marinade and seal.

3. Place the onions and peppers in another large food storage bag, pour in the rest of the marinade and seal. Place the steak and vegetables in the refrigerator, laying the bags flat and marinate for 4 hours, flipping the bags occasionally.

4. Prepare the grill for direct heat and preheat to medium-high.

5. Drain and discard the marinade from the steak and vegetables. Brush the grates with oil and cook the steak 2 to 3 minutes per side with the lid closed. Remove from grill, place on a cutting board, cover with foil and let sit for 10 minutes.

6. While the steak is resting, prepare the vegetables. Place a cast-iron skillet directly on the grill and let it heat. Add 1 Tbsp. of vegetable oil and let that get hot. Add the vegetables and cook, stirring occasionally, until softened, about 7 minutes. Alternately, you can cook the vegetables on the stove.

7. Slice the steak thinly and serve with the vegetables and warmed tortillas.

Barbara Sheldon, Lloyd Whitlock and John Wayne in *The Lucky Texan* (1934).

John Wayne in *The Shootist* (1976).

WILD WEST STRIP STEAK

Strip steak is a bit tougher than a cut like filet mignon, but it more than makes up for it with flavor. This quick preparation lets the grill do the work so you can take it easy for once in your life.

PROVISIONS

4   (14-oz.) strip steaks

   Extra virgin olive oil

   Smoked paprika

   Salt and pepper

PREP

1. Rub steaks with olive oil, mashing lightly with your palms. Liberally season steaks with as much smoked paprika, salt and pepper as you want; stick in the fridge, uncovered, for up to 24 hours.

2. Prepare your grill.

3. Toss your steaks on the grill over medium-high heat. Cook for 6 minutes and flip. Cook for 6 more minutes or to your desired degree of doneness.

BLACK-AND-BLUE STEAKS

Any villain who dared cross John Wayne's on-screen characters typically left the showdown black and blue—if they were lucky. A hard day of fightin' will work up anyone's appetite, and these Pittsburgh-style steaks—black char on the outside, rare temp within—will hit the spot.

PROVISIONS

2 (12-oz.) shell steaks

¼ tsp. salt

⅛ tsp. pepper

4 Tbsp. butter

PREP

1. The key to a good Pittsburgh steak is high heat. You want to sear the steak until it's crispy without cooking the meat through.

2. Heat your cast iron skillet over the grill until it's searing hot.

3. Season steaks with salt and pepper.

4. Add butter to the skillet, then toss in steaks. Cook for 5 minutes or until nice and crisp. When steaks stop sizzling, flip them. Cook for another 5 minutes.

5. Remove steaks from heat and let rest for 8 minutes before serving.

DID YOU KNOW?

To win a bet with longtime friend and co-star Ward Bond (below in 1944's *Tall in the Saddle*), John Wayne once punched him in the face through a closed door.

Duke and Ward Bond in *Tall in the Saddle* (1944).

STEAK-ING HIS CLAIM
Lee Van Cleef, Lee Marvin, James Stewart and John Wayne in *The Man Who Shot Liberty Valance* (1962). The film features the first instances of Duke using the iconic term "pilgrim."

John Wayne and his son Ethan on the set of *McQ* (1974).

BACON-WRAPPED FILET MIGNON

One of Duke's favorite foods, bacon tastes great on everything—including filet mignon. Wrapping these lean pieces of meat in bacon adds fat and flavor and traps in extra moisture.

PROVISIONS

- **4** **(10-oz.) cuts of filet mignon**
- **8** **slices bacon**
- **4** **Tbsp. olive oil**
- **Salt and pepper**
- **Fresh rosemary**

PREP

1. Heat grill to high.

2. Wrap two pieces of bacon around each filet, keeping the pieces even with the top and bottom of the steaks. Secure bacon with toothpicks.

3. Mix olive oil with desired amount of salt, pepper and rosemary. Massage into your filets, but be careful not to rip apart your bacon in the process.

4. Turn grill down to medium-high heat.

5. Put the steaks on the grill to sear. Close lid. After 3 minutes, flip steaks. Cook for 3 more minutes. Continue flipping steaks until done to your liking. Let rest for 10 minutes, then serve.

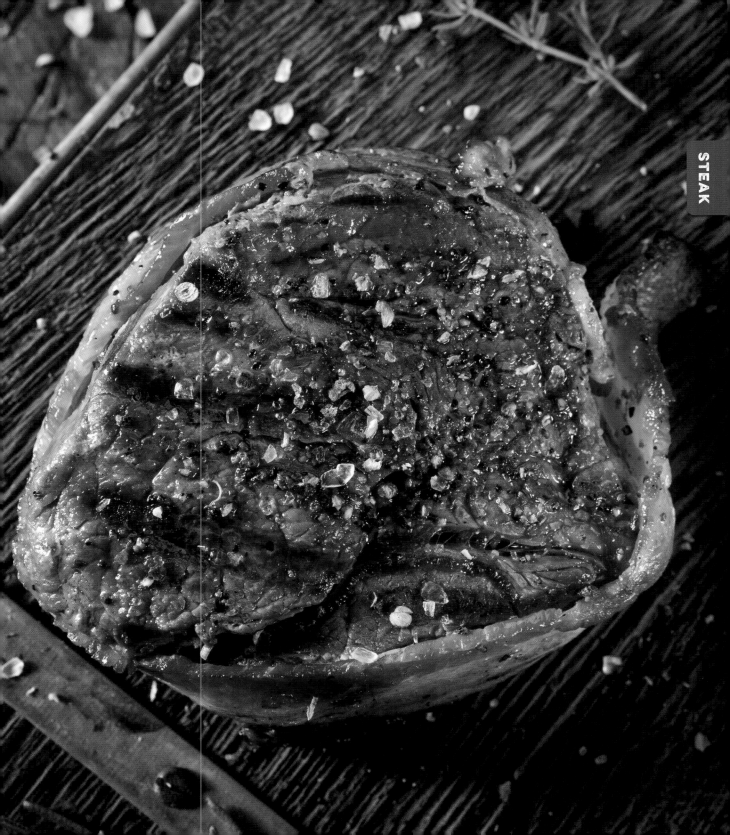

PEPPERED COWBOY STEAKS

A bone-in ribeye or "cowboy steak" is a can't-miss cut everybody can agree on. This simple rub of black and red ground peppers, lemon pepper, garlic powder and parsley flakes takes ribeyes from good to extraordinary. One hour in the fridge is all it takes to add even more flavor to these solid standbys.

PROVISIONS

2½ tsp. black pepper

1 Tbsp. dried thyme

1½ tsp. salt

4½ tsp. garlic powder

1½ tsp. lemon pepper

1½ tsp. ground red pepper

1½ tsp. dried parsley flakes

6 (1½-inch-thick) bone-in ribeyes

3 tsp. olive oil

PREP

1. Mix first seven ingredients. Brush steaks with oil; rub with pepper mixture. Cover and stick in the fridge for 1 hour.

2. Grill with grill lid shut, over medium-high heat for 8 to 10 minutes on each side or to desired degree of doneness.

WAYNE FAMILY TIP

A bone-in steak will always have a bit more flavor than a cut off the bone. You can cover any exposed bones on your steaks with aluminum foil to keep them from charring as you grill.

John Wayne as the iconic character Rooster Cogburn in *True Grit* (1969).

SPICE-RUBBED FLANK STEAK
WITH SPICY PEACH-BOURBON SAUCE

Canned peach nectar, near the bottled fruit juices in the grocery, is the base for a slightly sweet sauce. You can make and refrigerate the sauce up to a day ahead—but make sure to bring it to room temperature before serving.

PROVISIONS

SAUCE

- 1 tsp. vegetable oil
- ¾ cup chopped Vidalia or other sweet onion
- 2 cloves garlic, minced
- 1½ cups peach nectar
- 3 Tbsp. brown sugar
- 2 Tbsp. cider vinegar
- 3 Tbsp. bourbon
- 2 Tbsp. ketchup
- 1½ tsp. Worcestershire sauce
- ½ tsp. crushed red pepper
- 1 tsp. fresh lime juice

STEAK

- 1 Tbsp. brown sugar
- 1¼ tsp. garlic powder
- 1¼ tsp. ground cumin
- 1 tsp. salt
- 1 tsp. ground coriander
- 1 tsp. paprika
- ¾ tsp. dry mustard
- ¾ tsp. freshly ground black pepper
- 2 (1-lb.) flank steaks, trimmed

PREP

1. To prepare sauce, heat oil in a medium saucepan over medium-high heat. Add onion and garlic, sauté for 5 minutes or until tender. Add nectar, brown sugar and vinegar. Bring to a boil and cook until reduced to 1 cup (about 15 minutes). Add bourbon, ketchup, Worcestershire and red pepper; cook over medium heat for 2 minutes, stirring occasionally. Remove from heat and stir in the lime juice. Cool slightly. Pour the sauce into a blender and process until smooth.

2. Prepare grill to cook at medium-high heat.

3. To prepare steak, combine brown sugar and next seven ingredients (through black pepper); rub over both sides of steak. Place steak and cook 7 minutes on each side or to desired degree of doneness. Cut steak diagonally across grain into thin slices. Serve with sauce.

Same Ol' Duke

Winning an Academy Award for Best Actor didn't much change John Wayne. Of his Oscar-winning performance in True Grit *(1969), Duke said, "You can't eat awards. Nor, more to the point, drink 'em."*

HICKORY GRILLED TENDERLOIN

WITH SWEET AND SPICY STEAK SAUCE

This zesty sauce is also great with grilled pork or chicken. Major Grey's chutney is a chunky, spicy Indian condiment; look for it in the supermarket near the steak sauces.

PROVISIONS

SAUCE

- ⅔ cup ketchup
- ½ cup Major Grey's chutney
- ⅓ cup bottled chili sauce
- ¼ cup steak sauce
- ¼ cup Worcestershire sauce
- ½ tsp. hot sauce

BEEF

- 4 cups hickory wood chips
- 2 cups water
- 1 (3¼-lb.) beef tenderloin, trimmed
- 1 tsp. freshly ground black pepper
- ½ tsp. salt

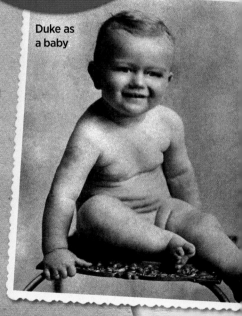

Duke as a baby

PREP

1. To prepare sauce, combine all six ingredients; cover and chill.

2. Soak wood chips in water for 1 hour.

3. Remove grill rack; set aside. Prepare grill for indirect grilling, heating one side to medium-high and leaving one side unheated.

4. Put half of the wood chips on hot coals. Place a disposable aluminum foil pan on unheated side of grill. Pour 2 cups water in pan. Grease up grill rack.

5. Sprinkle beef evenly with salt and pepper. Place beef on grill rack over foil pan on unheated side. Close lid; cook for 55 minutes or until a thermometer registers 135 degrees or to desired degree of doneness. Add additional wood chips halfway through cooking time.

6. Remove beef from grill. Cover lightly with foil and let stand for 15 minutes. Cut beef across grain into thin slices. Serve with sauce.

SKIRT STEAK
WITH CHIMICHURRI

Easy to find and quick to cook, skirt steak is an obvious choice for a spur-of-the-moment cookout. Add this hearty herb sauce for flavor and color.

PROVISIONS

½	**cup finely chopped fresh parsley**
⅓	**cup extra virgin olive oil**
¼	**cup fresh lemon juice**
2	**cloves garlic, finely chopped**
½	**tsp. crushed red pepper or more to taste**
	Salt
1½	**lb. skirt steak**

PREP

1. For chimichurri, mix parsley, oil, lemon juice, garlic, crushed red pepper and ¼ tsp. salt in a bowl.

2. For the steak, preheat your grill to high and oil when hot. Sprinkle steak with salt. Grill steak for 4 to 6 minutes, flip and continue to cook until the steak reaches your desired degree of doneness.

3. Transfer steak to cutting board, tent loosely with foil and let stand for 5 minutes. Slice and spoon chimichurri on top to serve.

Keeping Busy

Just one year after the release of his widely revered film The Searchers *(1956), John Wayne was not about to rest on his laurels. The year 1957 saw Duke star in three films:* The Wings of Eagles, Jet Pilot *and* Legend of the Lost.

Duke signs photos on the set of *Jet Pilot* (1957).

Duke with a gun originally made for the King of Belgium, c. 1955.

TENNESSEE T-BONE STEAKS
WITH WHISKEY BUTTER

T-bone steaks come from the short loin and have huge flavor. Often, this cut tastes best when you let that flavor shine through and don't clutter it up with a bunch of fancy seasonings. The whiskey butter is a side you can throw on the meat as a garnish or serve with fresh bread or biscuits. It's a meal fit for Davy Crockett.

PROVISIONS

STEAK

2 (1½-inch-thick) T-bone steaks

2 tsp. salt

1 tsp. black pepper

BUTTER

½ cup butter, softened

2 Tbsp. whiskey

1 Tbsp. white wine vinegar

1 Tbsp. Worcestershire sauce

2 tsp. Dijon mustard

¼ tsp. salt

¼ tsp. cayenne pepper

PREP

1. Bring grill to medium heat.

2. Cover both sides of your room-temperature steaks with salt and pepper. Put steaks on grill and cook for 9 to 11 minutes, flipping once.

3. For butter, mix all the ingredients together until well blended. Pack into a bowl using wax paper, cover and chill until you're ready to serve.

SPICY GRILLED SKIRT STEAK

It's hard to improve upon the beauty of a well-grilled steak,
but this recipe manages the impossible task with no muss or fuss.

PROVISIONS

- 4 Tbsp. brown sugar
- 2 Tbsp. kosher salt
- 2 Tbsp. smoked paprika
- 1 Tbsp. garlic powder
- 2 tsp. cayenne pepper
- 2½ lb. skirt steak
- Vegetable oil
- ¼ cup butter, melted

PREP

1. In a small mixing bowl, combine the brown sugar, salt, paprika, garlic powder and cayenne pepper. Press the mixture generously on both sides of the skirt steak. Let sit at room temperature while preparing the grill.

2. Prepare the grill for direct heat. Brush the grill grates with oil.

3. Pat the steak dry and grill for 2 to 3 minutes per side for medium rare. Cover the steak with foil and let sit for 10 minutes before slicing.

4. If using a grill pan, heat the pan until it is screaming hot, do not oil the pan, and grill as above.

John Wayne in *The Dawn Rider* (1935).

DID YOU KNOW?

In addition to *The Dawn Rider* (1935), director Robert N. Bradbury helmed several other Duke films in the 1930s, including *Blue Steel* (1934) and *Westward Ho* (1935).

CHIPOTLE FLANK STEAK

South-of-the-border spices help bring a new taste to a classic cut of meat.

PROVISIONS

- ½ cup orange juice
- ½ cup honey
- Juice of 2 limes
- ½ cup chopped cilantro leaves
- 3 garlic cloves, grated
- 3 Tbsp. Dijon mustard
- 1 chipotle in adobo sauce, minced, with 1 Tbsp. sauce
- 2 tsp. ground cumin
- 2 tsp. kosher or fine sea salt
- 1 tsp. pepper
- 1½–2 lb. flank steak
- 1 Tbsp. cold butter

PREP

1. Combine the orange juice, honey, lime juice, cilantro, garlic, mustard, chipotle in adobo sauce, cumin, salt and pepper in a mixing bowl and whisk together. Put the steak in a large food storage bag, pour in the marinade and let marinate at room temperature for 1 hour or in the refrigerator for 4 to 8 hours.

2. Remove the steak from the marinade, pour the marinade into a sauce pan, pat the steak dry, and let come to room temperature if refrigerated. Bring the marinade to a boil. Continue to boil the marinade while the steak cooks and rests until it reduces to ¼ cup. Take off the heat and stir in the butter until it melts.

3. Preheat a cast-iron grill pan over high heat for 5 minutes. Spray the pan with nonstick cooking spray. Place the steak on the hot grill pan and cook, undisturbed, for 4 minutes. Flip and cook for another 4 minutes or until desired doneness. Take off the grill pan and let rest 5 to 10 minutes before slicing. Slice the meat against the grain. Serve with the sauce, lime and orange wedges and fresh cilantro if desired.

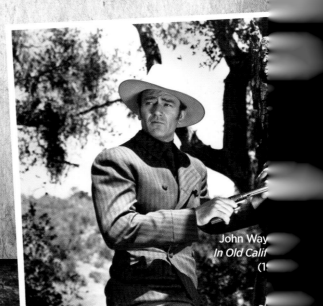

John Way
In Old Calif
(1

BUSINESS OVER A BITE TO EAT

Director Henry Hathaway, John Wayne and others sit down for a meal together. Duke and Hathaway made seven films together between the years of 1941 and 1969.

PERFECT PORTERHOUSE STEAK

Once John Wayne could afford steak, he never went back.
Once you try this steak, you'll never settle for less, either.

PROVISIONS

- 1 (2-in. thick) porterhouse steak
- Kosher or fine sea salt, to taste
- Pepper, to taste
- 1 Tbsp. vegetable oil
- 4 whole garlic cloves, peeled
- 4 sprigs fresh rosemary
- 3 Tbsp. butter

PREP

1. Remove steak from refrigerator and let sit at room temperature for 30 minutes.

2. Preheat oven to 500 degrees F.

3. Pat the steak dry with paper towels and season liberally with salt and pepper on both sides.

4. Heat a cast-iron skillet on the stove over medium-high, add the oil, garlic and rosemary and heat until the oil starts to smoke. Remove and discard the garlic and rosemary. Place the steak in the center of the pan and let it cook without moving it for 4 minutes. Flip the steak over, put the butter on top and place in the preheated oven. Let it cook for another 5 to 6 minutes or until it reaches an internal temperature of 125 degrees F (for medium-rare). Remove from the oven, take the steak from the pan and let it rest for 5 to 10 minutes before serving.

John Wayne and Katharine Hepburn in *Rooster Cogburn* (1975).

DID YOU KNOW?

Rooster Cogburn is the only time John Wayne starred in a sequel to one of his major motion pictures, and also the only time he worked with Katharine Hepburn.

DID YOU KNOW?

While it is now considered his signature term of endearment, John Wayne did not utter the nickname "pilgrim" on the silver screen until the 1962 film *The Man Who Shot Liberty Valance.*

GUNSLINGER STEAK SALAD

Add some beefy sizzle to this medley of veggies—it's what Duke would do.

PROVISIONS

- ½ cup plus 1 Tbsp. barbecue sauce, divided
- 5 Tbsp. olive oil plus more for brushing the vegetables, use divided
- 2 Tbsp. balsamic vinegar, use divided
- 2 lb. flank steak (approximately ¾-in. thick)
- Vegetable oil, for grill
- 2 romaine lettuce hearts
- 1 large radicchio
- 1 large red onion
- Kosher or fine sea salt, to taste
- Pepper, to taste
- 1 pint cherry or pear tomatoes

PREP

1. Combine ½ cup barbecue sauce, 2 Tbsp. olive oil and 1 Tbsp. balsamic vinegar and pour into a large plastic food storage bag. Add the flank steak, close the bag and flip several times to coat. Let marinate at room temperature for 20 to 30 minutes or in the refrigerator for up to 12 hours. (If marinating in the refrigerator, let sit at room temperature for 20 to 30 minutes before grilling.)

2. Prepare the grill for direct heat and preheat to medium-high. Brush the grates of the grill with oil. Remove the steak from the marinade and dry with paper towels. Discard the marinade. Grill the steak with the lid of the grill closed for 4 to 5 minutes per side for medium rare. Remove the steak from the grill, place on a platter and cover with foil. Let rest for 15 minutes.

3. While the steak is resting, prepare the salad. Cut the romaine hearts and radicchio into quarters, lengthwise. Slice the onion into ½-inch-thick slices. Brush with some olive oil and sprinkle with a little salt and pepper. Place the onions on the grill and cook with the lid closed for 5 minutes. Turn the onion slices over, add the lettuce and radicchio and cook for about 5 minutes (along with the onions) turning 3 or 4 times or until slightly wilted with some brown spots. Remove from grill and cut the lettuce into large chunks. Separate the onion rings. Whisk together the 3 Tbsp. olive oil, 1 Tbsp. balsamic vinegar and 1 Tbsp. barbecue sauce together in a large mixing bowl. Add the lettuce, radicchio and onions and toss to coat. Place on a platter. Slice the steak thinly across the grain and place on top of the salad. Scatter tomatoes around.

DID YOU KNOW?

Nearly 2,500 horses were used in filming *The Undefeated* (1969). John Wayne sustained a shoulder injury when he fell off one of his equine costars.

BLT STEAK SANDWICH

The classic sandwich goes from good to great once you add Duke's favorite ingredient: steak.

PROVISIONS

BACON MAYONNAISE

- 1 cup mayonnaise
- 6 slices bacon, cooked, crumbled and cooled
- 2 Tbsp. minced chives
- 1 tsp. red wine vinegar
- Salt and pepper, to taste

STEAK

- ½ cup olive oil
- ¼ cup red wine vinegar
- 2 Tbsp. Worcestershire sauce
- ½ tsp. kosher or fine sea salt
- ½ tsp. pepper
- 1½ lb. flank steaks
- Vegetable oil, for grill

SANDWICHES

- 6 hoagie rolls
- 2 tomatoes, sliced
- 1 cup baby arugula

PREP

BACON MAYONNAISE

1. Combine the mayonnaise, bacon, chives and red wine vinegar. Season to taste with salt and pepper. Refrigerate covered until ready to serve.

STEAK

1. Combine olive oil with vinegar, Worcestershire sauce, salt and pepper. Pour into a large food storage bag, add the flank steak and flip several times to coat. Let marinate at room temperature for 20 to 30 minutes or in the refrigerator for up to 12 hours. (If marinating in the refrigerator, let sit at room temperature for 20 to 30 minutes before grilling.)

2. Prepare the grill for direct heat and preheat to medium-high. Brush the grates of the grill with oil. Remove the steak from the marinade and dry with paper towels. Discard the marinade. Grill the steak with the lid closed for 4 to 5 minutes per side for medium rare. Remove the steak from the grill, place on a platter and cover with foil. Let rest for 15 minutes. Slice the hoagie rolls and lightly grill the cut sides for 10 to 20 seconds.

3. Thinly slice the steak across the grain.

4. Spread both sides of the hoagie rolls with the bacon mayonnaise. Top with steak, tomato slices and arugula.

John Wayne in *The Undefeated* (1969).

**FINGER-LICKIN'
FRIED CHICKEN**
PAGE 118

CHICKEN

If you're feeding folks who prefer white meat, these simple, delicious recipes will be good for your next feast.

GUN-SMOKEY BARBECUE CHICKEN

Help yourself to some high-caliber chicken with this recipe.

PROVISIONS

- 3 Tbsp. melted butter
- ¼ cup plus 3 Tbsp. Worcestershire sauce, divided
- 1 (3½- to 4-lb.) whole chicken, cut into 8 pieces
- Kosher or fine sea salt, to taste
- Pepper, to taste
- Vegetable oil, for grill
- 1 cup ketchup
- ½ cup brown sugar
- ½ cup honey
- ¼ cup apple cider vinegar
- 1½ tsp. garlic powder
- 1½ tsp. onion powder

PREP

1. Prepare the grill for direct and indirect heat and preheat to medium.

2. Combine the melted butter with 3 Tbsp. Worcestershire sauce and brush liberally on all sides of the chicken pieces. Season well with salt and pepper. Brush the grill grates with oil.

3. Place the chicken pieces skin side up on the indirect side of the grill placing the smaller pieces farthest away from the heat source. Grill for 20 minutes with the lid closed. Flip the chicken pieces, close the lid and grill for another 20 minutes or until the internal temperature reaches 160 degrees F.

4. While the chicken is grilling, combine the ketchup, brown sugar, honey, remaining ¼ cup Worcestershire sauce, apple cider vinegar, garlic powder and onion powder in a small saucepan. Bring to a boil over medium-high heat. Reduce heat and simmer for 10 minutes. Let cool.

5. When the chicken reaches 160 degrees F, brush with the sauce and move to the direct heat side of the grill. Cook for 4 to 5 more minutes, brush with sauce, flipping every minute or two. Serve any remaining sauce on the side.

John Wayne introduces the TV series *Gunsmoke* (1955).

WAYNE FAMILY TIP

If you end up with leftover pieces of chicken, you may want to forgo the grill the second time around. Reheating this chicken in the oven will give it a welcome crispy finish.

HOME ON THE RANGE CHICKEN

This juicy bird will have everyone running to the table—no dinner bell needed.

Duke and Buck Jones in *The Range Feud* (1931).

PROVISIONS

- 1 cup Italian parsley
- ¼ cup cilantro leaves
- ½ cup olive oil
- ¼ cup white wine vinegar
- 1 tsp. dried oregano
- 1 tsp. kosher or fine sea salt
- ½ tsp. pepper
- ½ tsp. red pepper flakes
- 8 boneless, skinless chicken thighs
- Vegetable oil, for grill

PREP

1. Place the parsley, cilantro, olive oil, vinegar, oregano, salt, pepper and red pepper in a blender and process until well blended, scraping down the sides as needed. Place ½ cup in a covered container and refrigerate until serving time. Pour the rest into a large food storage bag, add the chicken thighs, squeeze out the excess air, seal the bag and refrigerate 1 to 12 hours.

2. Prepare the grill for direct heat and preheat to medium-high.

3. Remove chicken from the bag, discarding any marinade. Brush the grill grates with oil and grill for 4 to 5 minutes per side or until the internal temperature reaches 160 to 165 degrees F.

4. Serve the chicken with the reserved sauce.

DID YOU KNOW?

Despite getting his first big break in *The Big Trail* (1930), John Wayne spent the 1930s starring in numerous low-budget, B-Westerns as he continued to hone his cowboy craft on screen.

NO-PUNCHES-PULLED CHICKEN

John Wayne could trade fisticuffs with the best of 'em, and this chicken is a satisfying smack in the tastebuds.

PROVISIONS

- 1 (3½- to 4-lb.) whole chicken, cut into 8 pieces
- 4 cups chicken stock or water
- 1 (15-oz.) can dark sweet cherries, undrained
- 1 cup ketchup
- ¾ cup pineapple juice
- 1 Tbsp. Worcestershire sauce
- 1 Tbsp. garlic powder
- 1 Tbsp. onion powder
- 1 tsp. (more if you like it spicier) chipotle chili powder
- 8 hamburger buns, toasted
  Coleslaw

PREP

1. Place the chicken in a saucepan or Dutch oven with the chicken stock or water. Bring to a boil, cover the pot, reduce heat to a simmer and cook until the chicken is cooked through, about 20 to 25 minutes. Remove the chicken from the liquid, let cool enough to handle then remove the skin and bones. Discard skin and bones and shred the chicken.

2. Puree the cherries along with their liquid in a blender and blend until smooth. Pour into a large saucepan and add the ketchup, pineapple juice, Worcestershire sauce, garlic, onion and chipotle chili powder. Stir to combine. Bring to a boil, reduce heat and simmer, uncovered, until thickened to the consistency of barbecue sauce, about 30 minutes. Add the shredded chicken to the sauce, stirring to combine.

3. Serve on toasted hamburger buns with a scoop of coleslaw.

Forrest Tucker and John Wayne in *Chisum* (1970).

DID YOU KNOW?

John Wayne's 1970 film *Chisum* was produced by his son Michael and released by the star's production company, Batjac.

OLD-FASHIONED BARBECUE CHICKEN PIZZA

Like seeing "John Wayne" on a movie poster, the appeal of this dish is right in the name.

PROVISIONS

Flour for rolling the dough

1 lb. pre-made pizza dough

Cornmeal

2 cups No-Punches-Pulled Chicken

½ cup barbecue sauce, divided

8 oz. fresh mozzarella cheese, sliced

¼ small red onion, thinly sliced

½ cup fresh cilantro leaves

PREP

1. Prepare the grill for direct heat and preheat to high.

2. Flour a work surface and roll the dough into a circle or rectangle. Sprinkle a generous layer of cornmeal on a flat baking sheet or pizza paddle. Place the rolled out dough on top.

3. Combine the chicken with ¼ cup barbecue sauce. Spread the remaining ¼ cup on the dough. Place the sliced mozzarella on the sauce, top with chicken and red onions.

4. Brush the grill grates with vegetable oil. Grill pizza for 4 to 5 minutes with the lid closed or until dough is brown and cheese is melted. Top with cilantro and serve.

DID YOU KNOW?

The year 1957 was a particularly busy one for John Wayne. The always-busy icon starred in three films that year: Legend of the Lost, Jet Pilot and The Wings of Eagles.

John Wayne in *Legend of the Lost* (1957).

89

John Wayne in the 1939 film *New Frontier.*

DID YOU KNOW?

Released shortly after his breakout role in *Stagecoach* (1939), *New Frontier* marked Duke's final outing as Stony Brooke in the *Three Mesquiteers* films.

MARINATED GRILLED CHICKEN LEGS

Soy sauce and fresh citrus juices deliver major flavor to tender chicken legs. With a dish like this, everybody's gonna want a drumstick.

PROVISIONS

- 1 **cup fresh orange juice**
- 2 **tbsp. fresh lemon juice**
- 4 **tsp. soy sauce**
- 1 **tbsp. dry sherry**
- 1½ **tsp. bottled garlic, minced**
- 1½ **tsp. balsamic vinegar**
- 1½ **tsp. basil oil**
- 1 **tsp. onion powder**
- 1 **tsp. dark sesame oil**
- ½ **tsp. salt**
- ¼ **tsp. hot pepper sauce**
- 8 **skinless chicken drumsticks (about 2¼-lb. total)**

Green onion strips (optional)

PREP

1. Put the first 11 ingredients in a large zip-top plastic bag. Add chicken to bag and seal. Marinate in refrigerator for 2 hours, flipping bag occasionally.

2. Prepare grill.

3. Remove chicken from bag, reserving marinade. Put reserved marinade in a small saucepan and cook over medium heat for 3 minutes. Place chicken on grill that's greased and ready to go; grill for 30 minutes or until chicken is done, flipping and basting occasionally with reserved marinade. Top with onion strips.

Duke and Al Ferguson in *Desert Trail* (1935).

WAYNE FAMILY TIP

Some people have an aversion to cilantro, so you may want to have an alternative on hand when serving these tacos. Shredded purple cabbage works well as a replacement.

DESERT TRAIL CHICKEN TACOS

It's no mirage—these delicious tacos are real and soon to leave you delighted.

PROVISIONS

CHICKEN

- 1 tsp. ground cumin
- 1 tsp. kosher or fine sea salt
- ½ tsp. pepper
- 1 lb. boneless, skinless chicken thighs
- Olive oil, for chicken

SALSA

- 1 lb. husked tomatillos
- 1 jalapeño pepper
- 1 small white or yellow onion, thickly sliced
- Vegetable oil, to taste
- 1 avocado
- 1 cup fresh cilantro leaves
- 4 Tbsp. lime juice (from 2 limes)
- Kosher or fine sea salt, to taste
- Pepper, to taste for serving

TACOS

- 8 corn tortillas
- 1 avocado, sliced
- 1 tomato, sliced
- Cilantro leaves
- Lime wedges

PREP

1. Prepare the grill for direct heat and preheat to medium-high.

2. Combine the cumin, salt and pepper in a small bowl. Brush the chicken thighs with olive oil and coat generously with the seasoning. Let sit at room temperature while preparing the salsa.

3. Coat the whole tomatillos, jalapeño pepper and onion slices with vegetable oil and place on the grill. Grill with the lid closed for 10 minutes, or until the vegetables are charred and soft, turning the vegetables a few times while cooking. Remove from grill and let cool slightly.

4. Cut the avocado in half, remove the seed but leave the peel on. Brush the cut sides with vegetable oil and place on the grill, cut side down, for 2 minutes or just until charred slightly.

5. Remove the stem from the jalapeño pepper and place in a blender with the tomatillos, onion slices and lime juice. Process until the salsa is chunky. Scoop out the flesh from the avocado and add to the blender with the cilantro. Pulse a few times to combine. Season to taste with salt and pepper.

6. Place the chicken thighs on the grill and cook with the lid closed 4 minutes per side or until cooked through. Let chicken rest for 5 minutes before slicing or chopping.

7. Lightly grill the tortillas.

8. Serve the tortillas with the chicken, salsa, avocado, tomato slices, cilantro leaves and lime wedges.

MANGO-TOPPED CHICKEN BREASTS

Cesar Romero, Elizabeth Allen, Jon Fong, John Wayne and Jeffrey Byron in *Donovan's Reef* (1963).

John Wayne once said, "A man oughta do what he thinks is best." In this case, covering chicken with downright delicious salsa fits the bill.

PROVISIONS

DRY RUB

- 2 tsp. chili powder
- 1 tsp. ground cumin
- 1 tsp. kosher or fine sea salt
- ½ tsp. pepper
- ½ tsp. cayenne pepper
- ¼ tsp. garlic powder
- ¼ tsp. onion powder
- Olive oil, for grill
- 4 boneless, skinless chicken breasts
- Vegetable oil, for grill

MANGO SALSA

- 2 ripe mangos, chopped
- ½ small red onion, finely diced
- ½ cup fresh cilantro
- 1 small jalapeño pepper, seeded, deveined and minced
- 4 Tbsp. lime juice

PREP

MANGO SALSA

1. Combine all the salsa ingredients together in a small bowl. Cover with plastic wrap and refrigerate until serving time. Can be made a day ahead.

CHICKEN

1. Combine all the rub ingredients together in a small bowl.

2. Prepare the grill for direct heat and preheat to medium-high.

3. Brush the chicken breasts with olive oil and apply the rub liberally on all sides. Can be grilled immediately or covered and placed in the refrigerator for up to 12 hours.

4. Brush the grill grates with oil and grill with the lid closed for 6 to 8 minutes per side or until the chicken reaches an internal temperature of 165 degrees F.

5. Serve the chicken breasts with the salsa.

WAYNE FAMILY TIP

If you want to add just a little more sweetness to your salsa, try switching out the red onion for a Vidalia onion. Prepare the same way you would the red onion.

DYNAMIC DINING DUO
Maureen O'Hara and John Wayne in *Rio Grande* (1950). Duke, O'Hara and director John Ford went on to make two other films together, *The Quiet Man* (1952) and *The Wings of Eagles* (1957).

GRILLED CHICKEN CAESAR SALAD

You won't regret digging into this mouthwatering salad for dinner.

PROVISIONS

- 2 tsp. garlic powder
- 2 tsp. kosher or fine sea salt
- 1 tsp. pepper
- Olive oil, for chicken
- 4 boneless, skinless chicken breasts
- 1 baguette
- Vegetable oil, for brushing
- 2 heads romaine lettuce
- 1 pint cherry tomatoes, halved
- ½ cup grated Parmesan cheese

DRESSING

- ¾ cup olive oil
- 1 Tbsp. mayonnaise
- 1 tsp. Dijon mustard
- 2 garlic cloves, minced
- ¼ cup lemon juice
- 1 tsp. kosher or fine sea salt
- ½ tsp. pepper
- ¼ cup grated Parmesan cheese

John Wayne in Rome, c. 1950s.

PREP

1. Prepare the grill for direct heat and preheat to medium-high.

2. Whisk the dressing ingredients together in a small bowl. Cover and refrigerate until serving time. Can be made a day ahead.

3. Combine the garlic powder, salt and pepper in a small bowl. Brush the chicken breasts with olive oil and apply the seasoning generously on all sides.

4. Cut the baguette in half lengthwise and brush both cut sides well with olive oil.

5. Grill the chicken with the lid closed for 6 to 8 minutes per side or until they reach an internal temperature of 160 degrees F. Put on a plate and let cool. Grill the bread with the lid open until lightly charred, about 2 minutes.

6. Chop the chicken and romaine lettuce. Place in a salad bowl with the tomatoes. Add the dressing and toss. Cut the bread into bite-sized pieces and add to the salad with ½ cup Parmesan cheese. Toss and serve.

SPICY GRILLED CHICKEN BREASTS

Things are just hotter in the West, including this delicious chicken recipe.

John Wayne in *The Spoilers* (1942).

PROVISIONS

- 4 bone-in, skin-on chicken breasts
- Olive oil, for chicken
- Vegetable oil, for grill

SPICE RUB

- 2 Tbsp. brown sugar
- 1 Tbsp. smoked paprika
- 2 tsp. kosher or fine sea salt
- 1 tsp. garlic powder
- 1 tsp. onion powder
- ½ tsp. chipotle chili powder

SAUCE

- 2 Tbsp. butter
- 2 Tbsp. honey
- 1 Tbsp. hot sauce

PREP

SPICE RUB

1. Combine all ingredients in a small bowl.

CHICKEN

1. Brush the chicken breasts with olive oil and rub liberally with the spice rub. Let sit for 15 minutes at room temperature.

2. Prepare grill for direct and indirect heat and preheat to medium-high.

3. Brush the grill grates with vegetable oil. Place the chicken breasts skin side up on the indirect heat side of the grill.

4. Grill with the lid closed for 15 minutes.

5. Flip the chicken and grill for 20 minutes or until an internal temperature of 160 degrees F is reached.

SAUCE

1. While chicken is grilling, heat the butter, honey and hot sauce together in a small saucepan.

2. When the chicken breasts have reached an internal temperature of 160 degrees F, brush with the sauce, move to the direct heat side of the grill and grill for 1 minute.

3. Brush with more sauce, flip and grill for another minute.

4. Remove chicken breasts from grill, brush with more sauce and serve.

WAYNE FAMILY TIP

For an added finishing touch of citrusy flavor, drizzle the juice of a lime over the chicken just before serving. You can also use lime wedges as a garnish when it comes time to plate the meal.

WESTERN BACON CHICKEN SKEWERS

When it came to grilling, Duke always believed the more meat, the better.

PROVISIONS

- 1 lb. boneless, skinless chicken breasts cut into 1-in. pieces
- 12 slices Canadian bacon, cut into quarters
- ½ pint cherry tomatoes
- Vegetable oil, for grill

MARINADE

- ½ cup mayonnaise
- ¼ cup buttermilk
- 1 Tbsp. lemon juice (from 1 lemon)
- ½ tsp. garlic powder
- ½ tsp. onion powder
- ½ tsp. kosher or fine sea salt
- ¼ tsp. pepper

CHIVE AIOLI

- ½ cup mayonnaise
- 1 garlic clove, minced
- 2 Tbsp. chopped chives

PREP

MARINADE

1. Combine the mayonnaise, buttermilk, lemon juice, garlic powder, onion powder, salt and pepper in a small mixing bowl and whisk well. Pour the mixture into a large food storage bag, add the chicken, squeeze out the excess air, seal the bag and refrigerate for 1 to 12 hours.

CHIVE AIOLI

1. Combine the mayonnaise, garlic and chives in a small bowl and whisk well. Cover with plastic wrap and refrigerate until serving time. Can be made a day ahead.

CHICKEN

1. Prepare the grill for direct heat and preheat to medium-high.

2. Remove chicken from the bag, discarding the marinade, and pat dry. Alternate the chicken on skewers with the Canadian bacon and tomatoes.

3. Brush the grill grates with oil and grill the skewers for 10 to 12 minutes with the lid closed, turning the skewers every 2 minutes.

4. Serve the skewers with the aioli.

John Wayne and Lloyd Whitlock in *West of the Divide* (1934).

CHICKEN KEBABS
WITH MUST-HAVE DIPPIN' SAUCE

Kebabs offer something for everyone. Your pals can pick and choose their favorite chunks of meat and veggies—but with this delicious recipe, they'll want it all, particularly when they taste the sauce you're serving up.

Raymond Hatton, Jack Mulhall, Francis X. Bushman Jr. and John Wayne in *The Three Musketeers* (1933).

PROVISIONS

- ½ cup canola oil
- ½ cup plus 1 Tbsp. lemon juice (from about 3 lemons)
- 4 tsp. cumin
- 2 tsp. ground coriander
- 2 tsp. paprika
- 4 cloves garlic, smashed
- 3 lb. boneless, skinless chicken breasts, cut into 1-inch pieces
- 2 red bell peppers, seeded, cut into 1-inch pieces
- 3 small zucchini, cut into 1-inch pieces
- 3 small summer squash, cut into 1-inch pieces
- 1 cup plain Greek yogurt
- 2 Tbsp. tahini
- 2 red onions, halved, each half cut into quarters
- Cooked brown rice (optional)
- Salt and pepper to taste

DID YOU KNOW?

John Wayne and Raymond Hatton were frequent co-stars in the early years of the legend's career. In addition to 1933's *The Three Musketeers*, Hatton also appeared with Duke in films such as *Reap the Wild Wind* (1942) and *Tall in the Saddle* (1944).

PREP

1. In a bowl, mix oil, ½ cup lemon juice, cumin, coriander, paprika and garlic; pour half into a separate bowl. Add chicken to one bowl; turn to coat. Toss peppers, zucchini and squash in the other bowl. Cover bowls and stick in the fridge for at least 2 hours.

2. To make sauce, whisk yogurt, tahini, 1 Tbsp. lemon juice and ½ tsp. salt in a bowl. Cover and chill.

3. Preheat grill to medium-high. Remove chicken and vegetables from marinade and pat dry. Thread chicken, vegetables and onions onto 12 skewers. Season kebabs with salt and pepper.

4. Grease up grill. Grill kebabs, flipping occasionally, until chicken is cooked through or 4 to 6 minutes. Serve over brown rice, if desired, with sauce.

GRILLED CHICKEN AND TWO-BEAN SALAD

This healthy, hearty chicken- and bean-filled salad is the perfect power meal for when you've worked up a Duke-sized appetite.

PROVISIONS

- ¾ lb. green beans, trimmed, cut into bite-size pieces
- ¼ cup extra virgin olive oil
- 1 Tbsp. Dijon mustard
- 1 Tbsp. red wine vinegar or sherry vinegar
- 1 small shallot, finely chopped (about 2½ Tbsp.)
- 1 pint cherry tomatoes, halved
- 1 (14-oz.) can white beans, drained
- 1 lb. boneless, skinless chicken breasts
- Salt and pepper to taste

PREP

1. Combine green beans and 1 cup lightly salted water in a microwave-safe bowl; cover. Microwave on high until beans are crisp-tender or about 4 minutes. Drain.

2. In a bowl, whisk 3 Tbsp. oil along with mustard, vinegar, ½ tsp. salt and shallots. Add green beans, tomatoes and white beans and toss until coated.

3. Preheat grill to high. Brush chicken with remaining 1 tablespoon oil; sprinkle with salt and pepper. Grill, covered, until chicken is cooked through, flipping once, 8 to 10 minutes total. Let cool slightly and chop.

4. Add chicken to the bowl with the rest of the ingredients, toss and serve.

WAYNE FAMILY TIP

Want to add a little flavor without using a heavy sauce? Smoke halved lemons over a low grill flame for 2 minutes and juice them into your salad dressing.

John and Patrick Wayne on the set of *Rio Bravo* (1959). Patrick's screen debut came in his father's 1950 film *Rio Grande*, in which he worked as an extra.

GRILLED CHIPOTLE CHICKEN QUESADILLAS

Grilling chicken adds a smoky flavor—the perfect complement to bold tastes of lime, cilantro and chile.

PROVISIONS

PICO DE GALLO

- 2 cups diced tomatoes
- ½ cup diced onion
- 2 Tbsp. minced jalapeño chiles
- ¼ cup minced fresh cilantro
- 2 Tbsp. fresh lime juice
- 1 tsp. garlic
- Salt

QUESADILLAS

- 4 boneless, skinless chicken breast halves
- 1 Tbsp. olive oil
- 1 canned chipotle chile in adobo sauce, drained and minced
- ¼ cup sour cream
- ¼ cup mayonnaise
- 1 Tbsp. lime juice
- 1 Tbsp. chopped fresh cilantro
- 8 (6-inch) corn tortillas
- 2 cups grated Monterey Jack cheese
- Salt and freshly ground black pepper

PREP

1. For pico de gallo, mix tomatoes, onion, jalapeño chiles, cilantro, lime juice and garlic in a bowl. Add salt to taste.

2. Brush chicken breasts with olive oil and sprinkle with salt and pepper. Place chicken on grill over medium heat or put chicken in a grill pan over medium heat. Cook for 4 to 5 minutes per side or until cooked through (cut to check). Slice cooked chicken breasts into ¼-inch-thick slices. Keep grill or grill pan hot.

3. In a small bowl, whisk together chipotle chile, sour cream, mayonnaise, lime juice and cilantro.

4. Spread 1 Tbsp. mixture on each of the tortillas. Top four of the tortillas each with ½ cup cheese and a quarter of the chicken slices, then cover with the remaining tortillas, sauce side down. Put each quesadilla on a dinner plate.

5. Slide quesadillas off plates onto the grill over medium heat or slide into a grill pan over medium heat (you may need to grill the quesadillas in batches). Grill uncovered, turning once, until cheese is melted and both sides are golden or about 2 minutes on each side (use a large spatula and tongs to flip the quesadillas). If grilling in batches, keep finished quesadillas warm in 200-degree oven until ready to serve.

6. Slice each quesadilla into wedges and serve with homemade pico de gallo on the side.

THE "KID" BECOMES A STAR

Clockwise from left: Donald Meek, John Wayne, Andy Devine (standing behind Duke), Claire Trevor, George Bancroft, Louise Platt, Tim Holt (standing beside Platt), John Carradine (standing next to Holt) and Thomas Mitchell (seated, far right end of table) in *Stagecoach* (1939).

GRILLED TEQUILA CHICKEN

Create an amazing blend of flavors by marinating the chicken in a mixture of lime juice, fresh ginger, dried chipotle chile and one of Duke's favorite spirits: tequila. You can also stir the marinade into whipped heavy cream for a rich, savory topping.

PROVISIONS

4 boneless, skinless chicken breast halves

½ cup garlic-infused olive oil

2 Tbsp. tequila

2 Tbsp. fresh lime juice

1½ tsp. hot sauce

1 tsp. Worcestershire

1 tsp. grated fresh ginger

1 tsp. ground dried chipotle chile

1 tsp. salt

⅓ cup heavy whipping cream

Cilantro (optional)

PREP

1. Pound chicken to ¼-inch thickness. In a bowl, whisk oil, tequila, lime juice, hot sauce, Worcestershire, ginger, chile and salt. Reserve ⅓ cup of marinade, then put the chicken in bowl, flip and marinate for 30 minutes.

2. Grill chicken over medium heat, flipping once, until cooked through or 6 to 8 minutes total.

3. In a small saucepan over medium-high heat, simmer reserved marinade until reduced to ¼ cup or about 2 minutes. Whisk in cream, then remove from heat. Serve chicken topped with sauce and cilantro.

More Than a Hobby

Duke's favorite way to pass the time was with a game of chess. Whether he was on set between takes, at home or relaxing on the Wild Goose, *he often had a game of chess going—sometimes with a glass of añejo tequila on the side. He even played correspondence matches via the post.*

John Wayne plots his next move in a game of chess on the set of *The War Wagon* (1967). The film paused production briefly to allow Duke to film commercials endorsing Ronald Reagan for governor of California.

GRILLED CHICKEN
WITH WHITE BARBECUE SAUCE

Tired of the same old sweet, tomato-based barbecue sauce? Try this Southern-style, tangy mayonnaise-based white sauce, and you may have a new favorite.

PROVISIONS

SAUCE

1½ cups mayonnaise

¼ cup white wine vinegar

1 clove garlic, minced

1 Tbsp. coarse ground pepper

1 Tbsp. spicy brown mustard

1 tsp. sugar

1 tsp. salt

2 tsp. horseradish

CHICKEN

1 Tbsp. dried thyme

1 Tbsp. dried oregano

1 Tbsp. ground cumin

1 Tbsp. paprika

1 tsp. onion powder

½ tsp. salt

½ tsp. pepper

10 chicken thighs (3 lb. total)

PREP

1. For sauce, stir together all sauce ingredients until well blended. Store in an airtight container in refrigerator for up to one week.

2. For chicken, combine first seven ingredients. Rinse chicken and pat dry, then rub mixture evenly over chicken. Place chicken in a zip-top plastic bag, seal and refrigerate for 4 hours. Remove chicken from bag.

3. Grill chicken, covered, over medium-high heat for 8 to 10 minutes on each side. Serve with sauce.

DID YOU KNOW?

Duke was first billed as John Wayne in the 1930 Western *The Big Trail*, in which he played rustic fur-trapper Breck Coleman. It was also his first leading role.

John Wayne on set of *The Big Trail* (1930).

CHICKEN THIGHS WITH CHIMICHURRI SAUCE

Duke liked things a bit on the spicy side. This chicken dish would have fit the bill nicely.

PROVISIONS

- **10** garlic cloves, peeled and roughly chopped
- **2** bunches flat leaf parsley
- **½** cup sherry vinegar or white balsamic vinegar
- **2** tsp. dried oregano
- **1** tsp. red pepper flakes
- **1½** cups plus 3 Tbsp. extra-virgin olive oil, divided
- **12** boneless, skinless chicken thighs
- Kosher salt and pepper, to taste

PREP

1. Put the garlic cloves and parsley in a food processor and pulse until finely chopped. Add the vinegar, oregano and red pepper flakes and process until combined. With the machine running, slowly drizzle in 1 ½ cups olive oil.

2. In a large plastic food storage bag, combine 6 Tbsp. of the sauce with the remaining 3 Tbsp. of olive oil. Add the chicken thighs and marinate at room temperature for 30 minutes or refrigerate for up to 12 hours. Reserve the rest of the sauce for serving. Remove the thighs from the marinade, pat dry and season with salt and pepper.

3. Heat a gas or charcoal grill to medium-high. Place the thighs over direct heat, close the barbecue lid and grill for 4 to 6 minutes per side or until the juices from the thickest part of the thigh run clear.

4. To serve, spoon some of the sauce over the thighs and serve the rest on the side.

John Wayne directs on the set of *The Alamo* (1960).

WAYNE FAMILY TIP

This sauce also pairs well with other grilled meats, such as skirt steak and pork chops.

FINGER-LICKIN' FRIED CHICKEN

When you cook this all-American classic to share with the ones you love, everyone's a winner.

PROVISIONS

3-4 lb. cut up chicken pieces

1 qt. buttermilk

3 large eggs

1 tsp. hot sauce

1 cup superfine white flour

⅓ cup cornmeal starch

1 tsp. kosher salt, plus more for seasoning

½ tsp. pepper, plus more for seasoning

1 tsp. garlic powder

1 tsp. paprika

Vegetable oil

PREP

1. Place the chicken pieces in a baking dish and pour on the buttermilk. Cover with plastic wrap and refrigerate for 2 hours or overnight. Remove the chicken from the buttermilk and pat dry with paper towels. Season liberally with salt and pepper.

2. Whisk the eggs together in a bowl with hot sauce.

3. In another bowl, whisk together the flour, starch, 1 tsp. salt, ½ tsp. pepper, garlic powder and paprika.

4. Dip the chicken pieces into the egg mixture then shake off the excess egg and coat well with the flour mixture. Push the flour into the chicken to coat well. Place on a plate and, once all the chicken is coated, let sit for 5 minutes. Coat the chicken in the flour mixture again.

5. Line a baking sheet with paper towels and place a wire cooling rack on top. Preheat oven to 200 degrees F.

6. Fill a large, deep frying pan or Dutch oven halfway with oil. Insert a frying or candy thermometer. Heat oil to 380 degrees F. Once the oil is to temperature, carefully lower the chicken into the hot oil, do not crowd the pan. Let cook for 4 minutes and flip over. Cook for 4 more minutes. You may have to adjust the temperature occasionally to keep the oil at 380 degrees F.

7. Remove the cooked chicken and place on the cooling rack, sprinkle with a little salt. Place in oven to keep warm while finishing up the rest of the chicken. Let the oil come back up to temperature and repeat with remaining chicken.

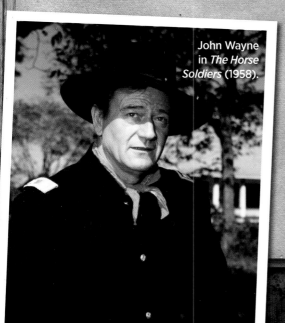

John Wayne in *The Horse Soldiers* (1958).

BRAISED CHICKEN THIGHS WITH ROOT VEGETABLES

This back-to-basics meal may surprise you with how quickly it becomes your new favorite.

PROVISIONS

- 2 tsp. paprika
- 1 tsp. garlic powder
- 1½ tsp. kosher or fine sea salt, plus more to taste
- ¾ tsp. pepper, plus more to taste
- 6 boneless, skinless chicken thighs, trimmed of excess fat
- 2 Tbsp. olive oil
- 1 large red onion, diced
- 1 lb baby red potatoes, scrubbed and cut in half
- ½ lb baby carrots
- ⅓ cup apple cider
- 2 Tbsp. flour
- 1½ cups chicken broth
- 4 thyme sprigs, plus more for garnish

PREP

1. Combine the paprika, garlic powder, 1½ tsp. salt and ¾ tsp. pepper in a small bowl. Coat the chicken thighs with the spice mixture.

2. Heat a cast-iron Dutch oven over medium-high for 3 minutes. Add the oil and let heat for a minute. Add the chicken thighs, in batches, and brown on both sides, about 4 to 5 minutes per side. Remove the chicken to a plate.

3. Add the onion and cook, stirring occasionally, until they begin to soften, about 5 minutes. Add the cider and cook stirring, until it is almost all evaporated. Add the potatoes, carrots and flour. Season with a large pinch of salt and pepper. Stir to coat the vegetables with the flour and cook for 1 minute. Gradually stir in the broth and bring to a boil, stirring frequently. Add the chicken along with any juices that have accumulated back to the pan. Add the thyme springs. Reduce heat to medium-low, cover the pan and let simmer until the chicken is cooked through and the vegetables are tender, about 25 minutes. Turn the chicken occasionally while it cooks. Taste and adjust seasoning with more salt and pepper if needed. Garnish with fresh thyme if desired.

John Wayne and Paul Fix in *Tycoon* (1947).

DID YOU KNOW?

Actor Paul Fix appeared in several of John Wayne's most famous films, including *Red River* (1948), *Hondo* (1953), *The High and the Mighty* (1954), *The Sea Chase* (1955) and *Blood Alley* (1955).

SKILLET CHICKEN POT PIE

Enjoy a new spin on an old favorite.

PROVISIONS

- 1 **premade pie crust**
- 1 **egg**
- 4 **Tbsp. butter**
- 1 **medium white or yellow onion, diced**
- 2 **medium carrots, peeled and diced**
- 3 **Tbsp. flour**
- 1½ **cups chicken broth**
- 1½ **cups milk**
- 3 **cups chopped cooked chicken**
- 1½ **cups frozen peas**
- **Kosher or fine sea salt, to taste**
- **Pepper, to taste**

PREP

1. Roll the crust between two pieces of parchment paper to about 1 in. larger than the top of your cast-iron skillet. Remove the top piece of parchment paper. Fold in the outer ½ in. of the dough and crimp to make an attractive border. Cut 4 slits in the center. Place the crust with the parchment paper on a baking sheet and refrigerate for 15 minutes.

2. Preheat oven to 400 degrees F.

3. Remove the crust from the refrigerator, whisk egg with 1 Tbsp. water and brush over the top of the crust. Bake until golden brown, 12 to 15 minutes. Remove from oven but leave oven on.

4. Melt the butter over medium heat in a cast-iron skillet. Add the onions and carrots and cook, stirring occasionally, until the onions soften, about 5 minutes. Add the flour and cook, stirring, for 1 minute. Add the chicken broth and milk and cook, stirring occasionally, until the sauce thickens, about 8 minutes. Stir in the chicken and peas, taste and season to taste with salt and pepper. Top with the parbaked crust and bake until the crust is deeply golden brown and the filling is bubbly, 10 to 15 minutes.

DID YOU KNOW?

John Wayne's 1934 film *Blue Steel* was a remake of the 1931 Western *A Son of the Plains*. Both were written and directed by the same filmmaker, Robert N. Bradbury.

John Wayne in *Blue Steel* (1934).

WAYNE FAMILY TIP

When the chicken is finished, be sure to avoid the urge to soak up the grease with paper towels. This can actually make the nice crispy finish turn soggy—and no one wants that!

THE FIGHTING KENTUCKIAN'S FRIED CHICKEN

This crispy chicken is worth fighting for (but luckily, you don't have to!).

PROVISIONS

- 3 cups buttermilk
- Kosher or fine sea salt, to taste
- 1 Tbsp. hot sauce
- 1 whole fryer chicken, cut into 10 pieces
- 2 cups flour
- 2 Tbsp. paprika
- 1 Tbsp. garlic powder
- 1 Tbsp. onion powder
- Pepper, to taste
- Vegetable shortening

PREP

1. Start this recipe the night before or early on the day you plan to serve the chicken. An instant read thermometer is useful not only for keeping the oil temperature correct but also for checking the doneness of the chicken.

2. In a large mixing bowl large enough to hold all the chicken, combine the buttermilk with 1 Tbsp. salt and the hot sauce. Add the chicken, stir to coat, cover the bowl with plastic wrap and refrigerate 8 to 24 hours.

3. Drain the chicken in a colander.

4. In a large paper bag, combine the flour, paprika, garlic powder, onion powder, 2 tsp. salt and 2 tsp. pepper. Shake to mix.

5. Add chicken (do not dry off buttermilk) to the bag, a few pieces at a time, and shake vigorously to coat. Place chicken on a board or plate and let sit while the shortening melts and heats.

6. Place a wire cooling rack over a sheet pan.

7. Put a large cast-iron skillet on the stove over low heat. Add enough vegetable shortening to come up ½ in. on the skillet. Let the shortening melt then raise the heat to medium and heat the oil to 325 degrees F. Fry the chicken in batches, making sure not to cover or crowd the pan. Fry until golden brown on both sides and the chicken has an internal temperature of 165 degrees F, 7 to 12 minutes per side depending on size. As the chicken pieces get done, place them on the wire rack to drain and sprinkle with a pinch of salt while still hot. Make sure the shortening temperature does not go above 325 degrees F or below 300 degrees F. Keep adjusting the heat as needed.

Duke in *The Fighting Kentuckian* (1949).

HONDO'S ROASTED CHICKEN

Whether you're a dispatch rider or a hungry ranch hand, this big bird is sure to satisfy.

PROVISIONS

- 1 (3½–4 lb.) whole chicken, giblets removed, rinsed and patted dry
- 4 Tbsp. butter, softened

  Kosher or fine sea salt, to taste

  Pepper, to taste
- 2 whole lemons, quartered
- 3 sprigs rosemary
- 1 large white yellow onion, sliced

PREP

1. Preheat oven to 450 degrees F.

2. Sprinkle the cavity of the chicken with salt and pepper. Stuff the lemon wedges and rosemary sprigs inside. Tie the chicken legs together with string. Rub the butter over the chicken, season with salt and pepper. Layer the onion slices on the bottom of a cast iron Dutch oven. Place the chicken on top of the onion slices. Roast for 45 minutes or until the juices run clear.

3. Let sit for 10 minutes. Untie the legs, remove the lemons and rosemary, and serve.

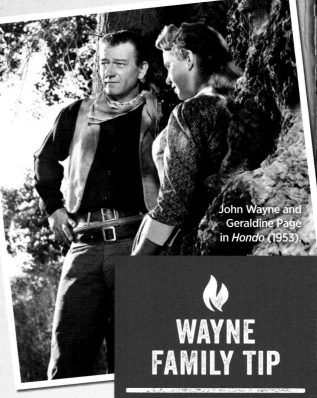

John Wayne and Geraldine Page in *Hondo* (1953).

WAYNE FAMILY TIP

The seasoning is the secret to this dish's deliciousness. You can create another layer of flavor by gently lifting the skin of the chicken when prepping to bake and adding a little more butter, salt and pepper.

SKILLET CHICKEN PARMESAN

Give this Old Country staple some new western sizzle—your guests will be glad you did.

PROVISIONS

- 2 boneless, skinless chicken breasts
- 2 large eggs
- ½ tsp. kosher or fine sea salt, plus more to taste
- ½ tsp. freshly ground black pepper, plus more to taste
- 1 cup panko style breadcrumbs
- ¼ cup grated Parmesan cheese, plus more for serving
- 1½ tsp. Italian seasoning, divided
- 1 tsp. garlic powder
- 4 Tbsp. olive oil, divided
- 2 Tbsp. butter, divided
- ½ cup marinara sauce
- 4 oz. fresh mozzarella cheese, grated
- 8 basil leaves, thinly sliced

PREP

1. Place the chicken breasts on a cutting board, place one hand on top and, with a sharp knife parallel to the cutting board, cut the breasts in half widthwise all the way through to create 2 halves of equal size per breast. Place each of the 4 breast halves between two pieces of plastic wrap and pound them out thinly with a rolling pin.

2. On a plate, combine the eggs with a large pinch of salt and pepper and whisk.

3. On another plate, combine the breadcrumbs, Parmesan cheese, Italian seasoning, garlic powder, ½ tsp. salt and ½ tsp. pepper.

4. Dip the chicken breast halves into the egg first then coat with the breadcrumb mixture, pressing the mixture onto the chicken breasts.

5. Position the top rack of the oven about 6 in. from the top and preheat the broiler to high. Line a baking sheet with parchment paper or a silicone baking mat.

6. In a large cast-iron skillet, heat 2 Tbsp. olive oil until hot over medium-high. Add 1 Tbsp. butter and once melted, add 2 of the coated chicken breast pieces. Fry for about 4 minutes per side or until golden brown. Place on prepared baking pan. Add another 2 Tbsp. of oil to the pan, let it heat up, add the remaining Tbsp. of butter, let it melt and cook the last two pieces of chicken the same way.

7. Spread marinara sauce over the chicken breasts, top with the mozzarella cheese and sprinkle the remaining ½ tsp. Italian seasoning over the top. Place under the broiler for about 2 minutes or until the cheese is melted. Top with the basil and serve.

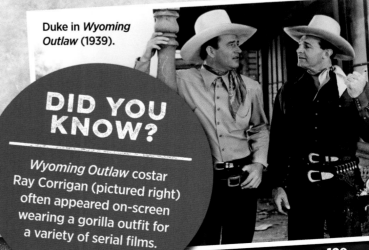

Duke in *Wyoming Outlaw* (1939).

DID YOU KNOW?

Wyoming Outlaw costar Ray Corrigan (pictured right) often appeared on-screen wearing a gorilla outfit for a variety of serial films.

THE DETECTIVE'S DINNER
John Wayne and Richard Attenborough in *Brannigan* (1975). Attenborough also had a prolific film career that spanned many decades and included classics such as *Jurassic Park* (1993).

CHICKEN ENCHILADA SKILLET

Your campfire meal just got a little hotter with this spicy classic.

PROVISIONS

- 1 tsp. ground cumin
- 1 tsp. kosher or fine sea salt
- ½ tsp. pepper
- 2 large boneless skinless chicken breasts (about ¾ lb.)
- 1½ Tbsp. olive oil
- 1 (10-oz.) can diced tomatoes and chilies, undrained
- 1 (10-oz.) can red enchilada sauce
- 4 cups corn tortilla chips
- 2 cups grated Monterey Jack cheese
- 1 avocado, diced
- ½ cup fresh cilantro leaves

PREP

1. Prepare the grill for direct heat. Place a cast-iron skillet on the grill and preheat the grill to medium-high (400 to 450 degrees F).

2. In a large mixing bowl, combine the cumin, salt and pepper. Cut the chicken breasts into bite-sized pieces and toss to coat well. Add the olive oil and stir.

3. Dump the chicken into the now preheated skillet, even out into a single layer and cook, stirring occasionally, until the chicken is cooked through, about 5 minutes.

4. Add the diced tomatoes and chilies to the skillet and cook for 1 minute, stirring. Add the enchilada sauce, stir and crush the tortilla chips into the skillet with your hands, breaking them into bite-sized pieces. Stir, cover the grill, and cook for 4 minutes. Stir, sprinkle the cheese all over the top, close the lid and cook for another 2 minutes or until the cheese has melted.

5. Let sit for 5 minutes off the heat. Sprinkle with avocado and cilantro, and serve.

John Wayne and others sing in a scene from *Westward Ho* (1935).

WAYNE FAMILY TIP

It can be frustrating waiting for a rock-solid avocado to soften. To speed up the ripening process, place your avocados in a brown paper bag, roll it shut and leave it on your kitchen counter two to three days prior to use.

ROSEMARY CHICKEN THIGHS
WITH SPINACH AND CHEESE GRITS

These sweet and spicy marinated thighs will wow even your most hard-to-impress guests. And if they don't like 'em, more for you.

WAYNE FAMILY TIP

Toss rosemary directly on your coals to add extra flavor to your food. Added bonus: the scent repels mosquitoes.

PROVISIONS

CHICKEN

- 1 clove garlic, pressed
- 1 Tbsp. olive oil
- 2 Tbsp. Dijon mustard
- 2 Tbsp. honey
- 1 tsp. salt
- 1 tsp. chopped fresh rosemary
- ½ tsp. pepper
- 1½ lb. boneless, skinless chicken thighs
- ½ lemon

SAUTÉED GARLIC SPINACH

- 1 Tbsp. olive oil
- 1 clove garlic, pressed
- 1 bag (10 oz.) fresh spinach

TWO-CHEESE GRITS

- 1 cup uncooked quick-cooking grits
- 1 cup (4 oz.) shredded cheddar cheese
- ½ cup (2 oz.) shredded Parmesan cheese
- 2 Tbsp. butter

PREP

1. Combine garlic and next six ingredients in a large heavy-duty zip-top plastic bag. Squeeze bag to combine ingredients. Add chicken, flip to coat and seal bag. Chill for at least one hour.

2. Preheat grill to medium-high. Remove chicken from marinade; discard marinade.

3. Grill chicken with lid down over medium-high heat for 5 to 7 minutes on each side. Transfer to a large piece of aluminum foil and squeeze juice from lemon over chicken; fold foil around chicken, covering chicken completely. Let stand 10 minutes.

SAUTÉED GARLIC SPINACH

1. Heat 1 tsp. olive oil in a nonstick skillet over medium-high heat. Sauté one pressed garlic clove in hot oil for 30 seconds.

2. Add spinach, thoroughly washed, to skillet and cook for 2 to 3 minutes or until spinach is wilted. Sprinkle with salt and pepper to taste. Serve spinach with slotted spoon or tongs. Makes four servings.

TWO-CHEESE GRITS

1. Bring 4 cups water and 1 tsp. salt to a boil in a 3-quart saucepan. Whisk in 1 cup grits; reduce heat to medium-low and cook for 5 to 6 minutes or until tender.

2. Remove from heat and stir in shredded cheddar cheese, shredded Parmesan cheese and butter. Salt and pepper to taste.

RANCHER'S FAVORITE CHICKEN

This is the meal you want to come home to after a hard day's work.

PROVISIONS

½ cup orange marmalade

½ cup olive oil

1 tsp. kosher salt

½ tsp. freshly ground black pepper

1¼–1½ tsp. chipotle chili powder, divided

12 boneless, skinless chicken thighs, trimmed of any excess fat

3 medium oranges, peeled and chopped

½ medium red onion, diced

2 plum tomatoes, seeded and chopped

¼ cup fresh cilantro, roughly chopped

1 lime, juiced

Vegetable oil, for grill

PREP

1. In a small mixing bowl, whisk together marmalade, olive oil, salt, pepper and 1 tsp. chipotle chili powder. Pour into a large food storage bag. Add the chicken thighs and marinate at room temperature for 1 hour or overnight in the refrigerator.

2. In a medium mixing bowl, combine chopped oranges, red onion, tomatoes, cilantro, lime juice and ¼–½ tsp. chipotle chili powder (depending on how spicy you want it). Reserve.

3. Heat grill to medium-high and brush the grates with oil. Remove the chicken from marinade and discard the marinade. Pat chicken dry and grill covered for 6 to 8 minutes per side. Serve with the citrus salsa.

Duke and his son Patrick at the 26 Bar Ranch.

HONEY MUSTARD PORK TENDERLOIN
PAGE 174

PORK

Whether it's sliced into bacon or shredded into barbecue, this versatile meat is practically its own food group.

Pan-Fried Pork Chops

Bacon-Wrapped Pork Tenderloin

Pan-Fried Pork Chops w/ Country Gravy

Sausage and Pepper Sandwiches

Sea Chase Sauerkraut Braised Bratwurst

Southern-Style Ribs

Pulled Pork Nachos

Pony Express Pulled Pork Sandwiches

Chili-Rubbed Pork Tenderloin

Paradise Canyon Pork Chili Verde

Prosciutto-Wrapped Grilled Pork

Big 'n Tasty Pulled Pork

Lentils and Sausage

Old Western Spicy Honey Ribs

Holiday Honey Ham

Honey Mustard Pork Tenderloin

Jerk-Style Ribs

Spicy Pork Skewers

Pork Tacos

Red River Ribs

Spiced Pork Patties

Mustard-Molasses Pork Chops

Beer-Soaked Spicy Ribs

Apricot Pork Chops

PAN-FRIED PORK CHOPS

There's nothing easier than throwing some chops in a skillet. Nothing tastier, either.

PROVISIONS

- **8** thin-cut bone-in pork chops
- **1** cup flour
- **1** tsp. kosher or fine sea salt
- **1** tsp. pepper
- **1** tsp. garlic powder
- **1** tsp. paprika
- **½** cup vegetable oil
- **2** Tbsp. butter

PREP

1. Dry the pork chops well with paper towels. Combine the flour, salt, pepper, garlic powder and paprika on a plate and mix well. Dredge the pork chops in the flour mixture and place on a clean plate. Let sit for 2 to 3 minutes then dredge them in the flour mixture again.

2. Heat the oil in a large cast-iron skillet over medium-high. Add the butter and let it melt. Fry the pork chops 2 to 3 at a time for 3 to 4 minutes or until golden brown. Flip and fry on the other side for 2 minutes or until golden brown and no pink juices remain. Keep warm while frying the rest of the pork chops.

Rock Hudson and John Wayne in *The Undefeated* (1969).

DID YOU KNOW?

John Wayne and Rock Hudson would often pass the time on set in between takes with one of Duke's favorite activities—playing chess!

PORK

BACON-WRAPPED PORK TENDERLOIN

Go ahead and pig out on this meal. You've earned it.

PROVISIONS

- 8 slices regular (not thick cut) bacon
- 1 (1–1½ lb.) pork tenderloin
-    Pepper, to taste
- 1 Tbsp. olive oil
- 2 Tbsp. honey

PREP

1. Place a cast-iron skillet in the oven and preheat oven to 350 degrees F.

2. Cut the bacon in half crosswise and lay the pieces next to each other on a cutting board, slightly overlapping each other. Sprinkle the pork tenderloin with a little pepper all over and lay on top of the bacon slices. Carefully fold the bacon up over the pork, securing with toothpicks if needed.

3. Carefully remove the skillet from the oven, place the oil in the pan and swirl the pan to coat the bottom. Place the pork in the skillet, brush with the honey and bake for 30 minutes or until the pork reaches an internal temperature of 140 degrees F, basting with the pan juices occasionally. Turn on the broiler and broil until the bacon on top is crisp, about 2 to 3 minutes. Baste the tenderloin again with the pan juice, cover loosely with foil and let rest 5 minutes before slicing and serving.

John Wayne in *The Train Robbers* (1973).

143

PAN-FRIED PORK CHOPS WITH COUNTRY GRAVY

This dinner delivers good old-fashioned flavor, just like you had as a young'un.

PROVISIONS

- 8 thin-cut bone-in pork chops
- 1½ cups flour
- 1½ tsp. kosher or fine sea salt, plus more to taste
- 1 tsp. pepper, plus more to taste
- 1½ tsp. paprika
- 4 Tbsp. olive oil
- 7 Tbsp. butter, divided
- 2¼ cups milk

PREP

1. Dry the pork chops well with paper towels. Combine the flour, 1½ tsp. salt, 1 tsp. pepper and paprika on a plate and mix well. Dredge the pork chops in the flour mixture and place on a clean plate. Let sit for 2 to 3 minutes then dredge them in the flour mixture again. Save 3 Tbsp. of the flour mixture.

2. Heat the oil in a large cast-iron skillet over medium-high. Add 4 Tbsp. butter and let it melt. Fry the pork chops in batches until well browned, about 2 to 3 minutes per side. Remove to a plate and keep warm.

3. Add 3 Tbsp. butter to the pan along with the reserved 3 Tbsp. of flour. Whisk until smooth and cook for 1 minute, whisking constantly. Add the milk and cook, whisking, until the gravy thickens, about 4 minutes. Taste and add more salt and pepper if needed. Serve the pork chops covered with the gravy.

DID YOU KNOW?

In addition to 1963's *McLintock!*, John Wayne and Bruce Cabot shared the screen in many other classics, including *Hellfighters* (1968), *Chisum* (1970) and *Big Jake* (1971).

John Wayne and Bruce Cabot in *McLintock!* (1963).

SAUSAGE AND PEPPER SANDWICHES

Tell your kin to grab a roll and get in line—these sandwiches are a hot item!

PROVISIONS

- 6 sweet or hot Italian sausages
- 1 Tbsp. olive oil
- 1 Tbsp. butter
- 1 medium white or yellow onion, thinly sliced
- 1 red bell pepper, seeded, deveined and thinly sliced
- 1 green bell pepper, seeded, deveined and thinly sliced
- 4 garlic cloves, minced
- 2 tsp. Italian seasoning
- 1 tsp. kosher or fine sea salt
- ½ tsp. pepper
- 6 hoagie rolls

PREP

1. Place the sausages in a large cast-iron skillet over medium heat and brown on all sides. Remove from the pan.

2. Add the oil and butter to the pan and heat until the butter melts. Add the onions and peppers and cook, stirring occasionally, for 2 to 3 minutes. Add the garlic and Italian seasoning, salt and pepper, and cook, stirring, for 30 seconds. Add the sausages back to the pan, turn the heat to low, cover with a lid or another skillet and cook until the peppers and onions are tender and the sausages are heated through, 10 to 15 minutes.

3. Serve the sausages on hoagie rolls with peppers and onions piled on.

DID YOU KNOW?

For his 1957 film *Legend of the Lost*, Duke collaborated with international star Sophia Loren and shot the film in Rome.

John Wayne takes a stroll through the streets of Rome, Italy.

147

SEA CHASE SAUERKRAUT BRAISED BRATWURST

Serve up these delicious links and you'll be the captain of the cookout.

PROVISIONS

- 2 Tbsp. vegetable oil
- 6 fresh bratwurst links
- 2 lb. red potatoes, scrubbed, unpeeled and cut into large chunks
- 1 large white or yellow onion, diced
- 3 garlic cloves, minced
- 2 Tbsp. brown sugar
- 1 lb. sauerkraut, drained
- 3 cups chicken broth
- 2 tsp. caraway seeds

PREP

1. Heat the oil in a large cast-iron skillet over medium-high. Prick holes in the casing of the bratwurst and add to the hot pan, brown well on all sides. Remove the sausages to a plate, add the potatoes and onions and cook, stirring occasionally, until they start to brown, about 5 minutes. Add the garlic and cook for 30 seconds, stirring. Add the brown sugar, stir to combine, then add the sauerkraut, chicken broth and caraway seeds. Bring to a simmer, reduce heat and simmer for 45 minutes.

Duke and Lana Turner in *The Sea Chase* (1955).

WAYNE FAMILY TIP

Dill may not be one of your go-to herbs, but it can be a great addition to any potato dish. Plus, the vibrant green sprigs will really add to the presentation when serving.

SOUTHERN-STYLE RIBS

A rack of ribs is to barbecue as John Wayne is to Westerns—hard to beat.

PROVISIONS

- 2 racks pork baby back ribs
  Vegetable oil, for grill rub
- ¼ cup dark brown sugar, packed
- ¼ cup paprika
- 1 Tbsp. kosher or fine sea salt
- 1 Tbsp. pepper
- 1 Tbsp. onion powder
- 1 Tbsp. garlic powder
- 2 tsp. dry mustard
- 2 tsp. cayenne pepper

PREP

1. Mix all rub ingredients together in a small mixing bowl.

2. Flip the ribs bone side up and insert a dinner knife just under the white membrane that covers the meat and bones. Gently peel the membrane off. Reserve ¼ of the rub mixture and coat the ribs with the rest. Wrap in foil and refrigerate 4 to 8 hours.

3. Preheat oven to 250 degrees F. Keep the ribs wrapped in foil, place on a baking sheet and bake in oven for 2 hours 30 minutes to 3 hours or until the ribs are tender.

4. Prepare the grill for direct heat and preheat to medium-high. Oil the grill grates. Remove the ribs from the foil, sprinkle with the reserved rub mixture and grill 7 to 10 minutes per side.

John Smith, John Wayne and Claudia Cardinale in *Circus World* (1964).

PULLED PORK NACHOS

These nachos will open your eyes (or eye) to a new world of deliciousness.

DID YOU KNOW?

John Wayne may continue to stand tall as America's most beloved actor, but the legend only has a single Oscar to his name—a Best Actor award for his work in *True Grit*.

PORK

PROVISIONS

- 6 oz. corn tortilla chips
- 2 cups warmed Pulled Pork (see page 165)
- 2 cups grated cheddar cheese
- ½ cup quick pickled red onions, drained
- ¼ cup pickled jalapeño pepper slices, drained

PREP

1. Position oven rack about 6 in. from the top. Preheat broiler to high.

2. Place tortilla chips on a heatproof platter or in a cast iron skillet. Top with pulled pork and cheddar cheese. Broil until the cheese is melted, 2 to 3 minutes.

3. Top with pickled red onions and pickled jalapeño pepper slices.

John Wayne in *True Grit* (1969).

153

A RANCHER READY TO EAT
From left: H.W. Gim, Chill Wills, John Wayne, Yvonne De Carlo and Patrick Wayne in *McLintock!* (1963). Duke's daughter Aissa, seen in the background, appears as an extra in the film.

PONY EXPRESS PULLED PORK SANDWICHES

Grab one of these mouth-watering sammies
to keep you full on the go.

PROVISIONS

4–5 cups hot Pulled Pork (see recipe page 165)

8 hamburger buns or Kaiser rolls,
lightly toasted or grilled

COLESLAW

1 small head green cabbage or 1 (16-oz.)
bag coleslaw mix

¼ cup mayonnaise

2 Tbsp. apple cider vinegar

1 Tbsp. sugar

1 tsp. kosher or fine sea salt

½ tsp. pepper

PREP

1. Combine all coleslaw ingredients in a medium
mixing bowl. Cover and refrigerate for 30
minutes for best flavor or serve immediately.

2. Place a heaping ½ cup of pulled pork
on the bottom bun, top with coleslaw and
top bun.

John Wayne in *Angel
and the Badman* (1947).

PORK

WAYNE FAMILY TIP

Feel free to leave out the mayonnaise in the coleslaw if you have guests who don't enjoy the spread's rich taste. The slaw will still be delicious.

CHILI-RUBBED PORK TENDERLOIN

A great cut of pork seasoned in a savory rub
is the right way to end a long day.

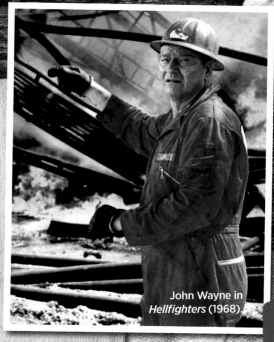

John Wayne in
Hellfighters (1968).

PROVISIONS

  1 (1¼- to 1½-lb.) pork tenderloin

CHILI RUB

  1½ tsp. chili powder

  ½ tsp. ground cumin

  ½ tsp. garlic powder

  ½ tsp. kosher or fine sea salt

  ¼ tsp. pepper

CORN AND AVOCADO SALSA

  1½ tsp. chili powder

  ½ tsp. ground cumin

  1 cup frozen corn kernels, thawed

  1 large tomato,
     seeded and chopped

  1 avocado, diced

  ½ cup diced red onion

  ½ cup cilantro leaves

  2 tbsp. lime juice (from 1 lime)

PREP

RUB

1. Combine all rub ingredients together in a small bowl.

2. Rub seasoning all over the pork. Wrap in plastic wrap and refrigerate for 30 minutes to 8 hours. Remove from refrigerator 20 minutes before grilling.

SALSA

1. Combine all salsa ingredients in a small bowl. Refrigerate covered until serving time.

PORK

1. Prepare grill for direct heat and preheat to medium-high. Grill the pork for 10 to 12 minutes or until it reaches an internal temperature of 140 degrees F, turning every 2 minutes.

2. Let pork sit 5 to 10 minutes before slicing. Serve with salsa.

DID YOU KNOW?

In addition to 1968's *Hellfighters*, Vera Miles also starred with John Wayne in *The Searchers* (1956), *The Man Who Shot Liberty Valance* (1962) and *The Green Berets* (1968).

PARADISE CANYON PORK CHILI VERDE

Don't accept counterfeit versions of the classics—this recipe is the real deal.

John Wayne and Yakima Canutt in *Paradise Canyon* (1935).

PROVISIONS

2	tsp. ground cumin	2	tsp. smoked paprika
1½	tsp. kosher or fine sea salt	4	cups vegetable or chicken stock
1	tsp. pepper	2	cups cilantro leaves, divided
2	lb. pork tenderloin	1	bunch green onions, trimmed and roughly chopped
2	Tbsp. olive or vegetable oil		
1	large white or yellow onion, diced	1	lb. Yukon gold potatoes, diced
4	garlic cloves, minced	1	lime, juiced
1	jalapeño pepper, deveined, seeded and minced		Lime wedges and corn tortillas for serving
1½	lb. tomatillos, husk removed, rinsed and chopped		
2	tsp. dried oregano		

PREP

1. Combine the cumin, salt and pepper in a medium mixing bowl. Cut the tenderloin into 1-in. pieces and add to the spice mixture. Toss well to coat.

2. Heat the oil in a large stock pot or Dutch oven over medium-high. Add the pork and cook, stirring occasionally, until the pork is browned on all sides, about 6 to 8 minutes. Remove the pork from the pot, place in a bowl and set aside. Add the onions and cook, stirring occasionally, until softened and starting to brown, about 5 minutes. Add the garlic and jalapeño and cook, stirring for 1 minute. Add the tomatillos, oregano and paprika and cook, stirring occasionally, until the tomatillos soften, about 5 minutes. Return the pork along with any juices that have accumulated back into the pot.

3. Combine the stock, 1½ cups cilantro and the green onions in a blender and puree. Pour the mixture into the pot, bring to a boil, reduce heat, cover and simmer for 30 minutes. Add the potatoes and simmer another 30 minutes or until the pork and potatoes are fork tender. Add the lime juice and adjust seasoning with more salt and pepper if needed. Just before serving, stir in the remaining ½ cup cilantro leaves.

4. Serve with lime wedges and corn tortillas.

WAYNE FAMILY TIP

The best thing about pork chili verde is its versatility. If you and your guests prefer, you can serve this dish poured over a bed of rice and beans rather than as a stew.

PROSCIUTTO-WRAPPED GRILLED PORK

What's the only way to make a pork dish better? By adding more pork.

PROVISIONS

APPLE COMPOTE

1	Tbsp. butter
2	large apples, cored and chopped
¼	cup dried cherries or cranberries
2	Tbsp. sugar
¼	tsp. kosher or fine sea salt
2	Tbsp. balsamic vinegar

PORK

1	(1- to 1 ½-lb.) pork tenderloin
	Garlic powder, to taste
	Pepper, to taste
6	oz. prosciutto, very thinly sliced
	Vegetable oil, for grill

PREP

APPLE COMPOTE

1. In a medium saucepan over medium heat, melt the butter. Add the apples, cherries or cranberries, sugar and salt. Toss to coat. Cover the pot and cook gently for about 15 minutes or until the apples and cherries or cranberries are tender. Remove the lid, raise the heat and bring the mixture to a boil. Add the vinegar and cook, stirring, until all liquid has evaporated. Let cool. Can be made up to a week in advance. Store covered in the refrigerator. Let come to room temperature before serving.

PORK

1. Prepare the grill for direct and indirect heat and preheat to medium.

2. Sprinkle all sides of pork with garlic powder and pepper. Lay the prosciutto slices next to each other on a cutting board. Place the tenderloin on top of the prosciutto and fold the prosciutto over pressing firmly. Brush grill grates with oil. Place the pork over direct heat and grill about 3 minutes per side or until the prosciutto is crispy. Move the pork to the indirect side of the grill and grill with the lid closed for another 10 to 12 minutes or until the pork reaches an internal temperature of 140 degrees F. Let sit for 5 minutes before slicing.

3. Serve the pork with the compote.

John Wayne in *The Man Who Shot Liberty Valance* (1962).

PORK

DID YOU KNOW?

While "pilgrim" is now synonymous with John Wayne, the term was only uttered by Duke in two films: *The Man Who Shot Liberty Valance* (1962) and *McLintock!* (1963).

Duke in a promo shot for *The Big Stampede* (1932).

DID YOU KNOW?

John Wayne didn't just play a cowboy in the movies—he also owned a livestock ranch in Arizona. Every year around Thanksgiving, he would host a large cattle sale.

BIG 'N' TASTY PULLED PORK

Don't you dare let anyone tell you one helping is enough of this recipe.

PROVISIONS

Vegetable oil, for slow cooker

1 (5- to 6-lb.) pork butt roast

2 cups cola

PORK RUB

½ cup brown sugar

¼ cup sugar

¼ cup kosher salt

2 Tbsp. chili powder

2 tsp. onion powder

2 tsp. garlic powder

2 tsp. paprika

1 tsp. pepper

BARBECUE SAUCE

1 cup cola (not diet)

1 cup ketchup

¼ cup Worcestershire sauce

2 Tbsp. apple cider vinegar

2 Tbsp. pork rub

PREP

RUB

1. Combine all rub ingredients in a small bowl. Reserve 2 Tbsp. for the sauce. Rub the rest of the seasoning on the pork.

PORK

1. Lightly grease a 6-lb. slow cooker with oil. Place the pork roast in the slow cooker, add 2 cups cola, cover and cook on low for 8 to 10 hours.

BARBECUE SAUCE

1. Combine all ingredients and 2 tbsp. of rub in a medium sauce pan. Bring to a boil over medium heat. Reduce heat and simmer gently, stirring occasionally, for 6 to 8 minutes or until slightly reduced. Let cool. Can be made ahead and stored in the refrigerator, covered, for up to 2 weeks.

2. When the pork is done, remove from the slow cooker and drain the cooking liquid. Shred the pork with 2 forks, return to slow cooker along with the barbecue sauce. Cook on low, covered, for about 15 minutes or until heated through.

LENTILS AND SAUSAGE

It doesn't matter how hungry they are—this hearty dish will keep them satisfied.

PROVISIONS

- 2 Tbsp. olive oil
- 1 white or yellow onion, chopped
- 2 carrots, diced
- 1 celery rib, diced
- 3 garlic cloves, minced
- 1 package lentil soup mix
- 6 cups water
- 4 Italian sausages
- 1 bunch kale, ribs removed, leaves coarsely chopped
- 2 Tbsp. balsamic vinegar
- Hot sauce, to taste
- Kosher salt and pepper, to taste

PREP

1. In a large Dutch oven or soup pot, heat the olive oil over medium-high. Add the onions, carrots and celery and cook until they start to soften, about 5 minutes. Add the garlic and cook for 30 seconds.

2. Rinse and pick over the lentils. Add to the pot along with the enclosed seasoning packet and 6 cups water. Bring to a boil, cover the pan, reduce heat to low and simmer for 30 minutes.

3. Heat a medium skillet over medium-high. Prick the skins of the Italian sausage and brown the sausages on all sides, about 5 to 6 minutes. Add about ¼ inch of water to the skillet, cover the skillet and reduce heat to medium. Cook until the sausages are cooked through, 10 to 15 minutes. Cover with foil to keep warm.

4. After the lentils have simmered for 30 minutes, remove the cover on the pan, stir in the kale and vinegar and cook until the kale is wilted and the lentils are tender, about 10 minutes. If you want your lentils soupier, you can add more water. Taste the lentils and season with salt, pepper and hot sauce. Slice the sausages diagonally and serve on top of the lentils.

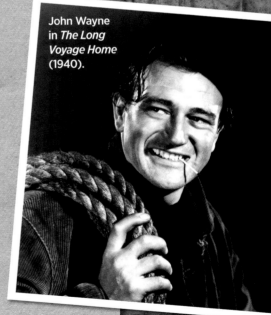

John Wayne in *The Long Voyage Home* (1940).

CHOWING DOWN WITH TROOPS
John Wayne during a visit to U.S. Army Special Forces facilities in Okinawa, Japan, c. 1966. The legend was scouting sites for shooting what would become *The Green Berets* (1967).

OLD WESTERN SPICY HONEY RIBS

The sweet and tangy taste of these juicy ribs will remain on your mind long after you've picked the bones clean.

PROVISIONS

- 2 slabs (about 3 lb.) baby back ribs
- Kosher or fine sea salt, to taste
- Pepper, to taste
- 1 cup honey
- ¼ cup tamari or soy sauce
- ¼ cup Dijon mustard
- 5 Tbsp. Sriracha sauce
- 2 tsp. dry ginger
- 2 limes, juiced

PREP

1. Preheat oven to 325 degrees F.

2. Flip the ribs bone side up and insert a dinner knife just under the white membrane that covers the meat and bones. Gently peel the membrane off. Season the ribs on all sides generously with salt and pepper.

3. Wrap each rack of ribs with heavy duty foil. Place on a baking sheet and bake for 2 hours 30 minutes to 3 hours or until the meat is tender.

4. While the ribs are cooking, combine the honey, tamari, mustard, Sriracha, ginger and lime juice in a saucepan. Bring to a boil. Reduce heat and let simmer until the mixture is reduced by half, about 10 minutes.

5. When the ribs have finished baking, remove from the oven, place the top rack about 8 inches from the broiler, and preheat the broiler to high.

6. Line 1–2 baking sheets with foil. Unwrap the ribs and place the ribs bone side down on the baking sheets. Brush with the sauce and broil 3 minutes. Brush with more sauce and broil another 2 to 3 minutes.

7. Serve the ribs with any extra sauce on the side.

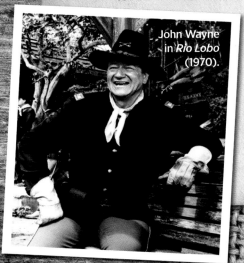

John Wayne in *Rio Lobo* (1970).

DID YOU KNOW?

Rio Lobo (1970) was the last collaboration between Duke and famed director Howard Hawks, who previously worked with John Wayne on *Red River* (1948), *Rio Bravo* (1959), *Hatari!* (1962) and *El Dorado* (1966).

HOLIDAY HONEY HAM

This main course will have you lamenting that Christmas only comes once a year. There's always New Year's Day.

PROVISIONS

1 (6- to 7-lb.) bone-in spiral-cut ham

¼ cup honey

¼ cup spicy brown mustard

¼ tsp. ground ginger

¼ tsp. ground cloves

¼ tsp. ground cinnamon

1 orange, juiced

1 lemon, juiced

1 lime, juiced

1 cup ginger ale

PREP

1. Use a 6-quart slow cooker. Unwrap the ham. If there is a flavor packet included, discard it. Place the ham into the slow cooker insert (flat side down).

2. In a small bowl, combine the honey, mustard, ginger, cloves and cinnamon. Smear this paste on top of the ham, allowing some to drip between the slices. Add all of the citrus juice and a little bit of the pulp to the empty mustard sauce bowl. Stir to combine. Pour this into the slow cooker.

3. Add the ginger ale. Cover and cook on low for 6 hours or on high for about 3 hours.

DID YOU KNOW?

Duke loved Christmas and would spend hours picking out gifts for his loved ones. Occasionally, the legend would even dress up as Santa Claus!

John Wayne celebrates Christmas with wife Pilar and children Aissa and Ethan.

HONEY MUSTARD PORK TENDERLOIN

This succulent pork tenderloin is marinated in a delicious honey-mustard sauce, a Carolina pairing fit for eating anywhere in the country.

PROVISIONS

- 2½ lb. pork tenderloin
- ½ cup chopped fresh parsley
- ½ cup red wine vinegar
- ¼ cup olive oil
- ¼ cup honey
- 3 Tbsp. country-Dijon mustard
- 2 cloves garlic, minced
- 1 Tbsp. kosher salt
- 1½ tsp. coarsely ground pepper

PREP

1. Remove silver skin from tenderloin, leaving a thin layer of fat covering the tenderloin.

2. Stir together chopped parsley and the next 7 ingredients until blended. Pour mixture in a large, shallow dish or zip-top plastic bag; add pork, cover or seal and chill for at least 2 hours and up to 8 hours, flipping occasionally. Remove pork, discarding marinade.

3. Heat grill to medium-high. Grill tenderloin with grill lid closed for 8 to 10 minutes, flipping once. Let rest for 10 minutes, then slice and serve.

JERK-STYLE RIBS
WITH STICKY RUM BBQ SAUCE

Get a taste of the islands by topping your baby back ribs with spicy jerk seasoning, marinating them in rum, then basting them with a tangy brown sugar and rum sauce.

John Wayne and his wife Pilar.

PROVISIONS

SAUCE

- 1 cup firmly packed dark or light brown sugar
- ½ cup ketchup
- ½ cup dark rum
- 1 Tbsp. jerk seasoning blend
- 1 tsp. lime zest
- 2 Tbsp. fresh lime juice
- 2 Tbsp. soy sauce
- 1 tsp. grated fresh ginger
- 2 cloves garlic, minced

RIBS

- 2 (2-lb.) racks baby back pork ribs
- 1 Tbsp. jerk seasoning blend
- 1 cup dark or spiced rum

PREP

1. For sauce, combine all ingredients in a saucepan over medium heat. Simmer for 5 to 7 minutes or until slightly thickened. Remove from heat and let sauce cool; refrigerate, covered, for up to 2 weeks.

2. Rinse and pat ribs dry. Rub ribs evenly with jerk seasoning.

3. Pour rum in zip-top plastic bag and add ribs, turning to coat. Seal and refrigerate for 1 hour, flipping every so often.

4. Light one side of grill, heating to medium. Place a drip pan beneath unlit side. Remove ribs from marinade, let drain quickly and place on grate above drip pan. Grill with lid closed, flipping occasionally, for 2½ to 3 hours or until ribs are browned and tender and meat has shrunk back from bones.

DID YOU KNOW?

Rum's got nothing on John Wayne. To date, the priciest case of the spirit sold for $128,000; the beret John Wayne wore in *The Green Berets* sold for $179,250.

PORK

SPICY PORK SKEWERS

If dinner needs to be done in a hurry, break out this simple, no-nonsense pork dish. You'll be good to go just a few minutes after the grill's fired up.

PROVISIONS

1¼   lb. ground pork

1½   Tbsp. minced garlic

 2   tsp. ground cumin

 2   tsp. ground paprika

 ⅓   cup finely chopped onion

1½   tsp. salt

 1   tsp. freshly ground black pepper

PREP

1. In a medium bowl, stir together the pork, garlic, cumin, paprika, onion, salt and pepper. Form into meatballs, each about the size of a golf ball, then thread the meat onto the skewers.

2. Lay skewers over medium coals. (If you are cooking with gas, close the lid.) Cook, turning once, for about 8 minutes or until browned on both sides and no longer pink in the center. Serve warm.

DID YOU KNOW?

Duke and his *The War Wagon* (1967) co-star Kirk Douglas were close pals who would play chess between takes and exchange letters when they weren't working together.

PORK

John Wayne in *The War Wagon* (1967).

PORK TACOS
WITH SUMMER SALSA

These grilled pork tacos are the perfect mix of flavor and presentation that'll have your friends thinking you must have been working in the kitchen all day.

PROVISIONS

- 2 Tbsp. fresh lime juice, divided
- 1½ Tbsp. extra virgin olive oil, divided
- 4 (4-oz.) boneless center-cut loin pork chops
- ¾ tsp. salt, divided
- ½ tsp. ground cumin
- ¼ tsp. freshly ground black pepper
- 1 clove garlic, minced
- 1 ear shucked corn
- ¼ cup diced red bell pepper
- ½ cup diced ripe nectarine
- ½ tsp. grated lime rind
- 1 seeded jalapeño pepper, minced
- 8 (6-inch) corn tortillas
- 1 cup shredded cabbage

PREP

1. Heat grill to medium-high heat.

2. Combine 2 tsp. lime juice, 1 Tbsp. oil and pork in a zip-top plastic bag and seal. Marinate for 10 minutes at room temperature. Remove pork from bag and discard marinade. Sprinkle both sides of pork with ½ tsp. salt, cumin, pepper and garlic. Put pork on a greased grill rack and grill for 3 minutes on each side or to desired degree of doneness. Let stand for 5 minutes. Slice pork into strips.

3. Lightly coat corn with cooking spray. Place corn on a lightly greased grill rack and grill for 6 minutes or until lightly charred, turning occasionally. Let corn stand for 5 minutes; cut kernels from cob. Combine kernels, 2 tsp. juice, remaining 1½ tsp. oil, remaining ¼ tsp. salt, bell pepper and next 3 ingredients (through jalapeño) in a bowl and toss to make salsa.

4. Put tortillas on a lightly greased grill rack and grill for 1 minute on each side or until lightly browned. Toss cabbage with remaining 2 tsp. lime juice. Place 2 tortillas on each of 4 plates and divide pork among tortillas. Top each taco with about 1 Tbsp. cabbage mixture and about 2 Tbsp. salsa.

Dynamic Duo

Though they only ended up sharing the screen in two films, Duke and Robert Mitchum proved a winning pair both as cowboys in El Dorado *(1966, pictured) and American soldiers in* The Longest Day *(1962).*

John Wayne and
Montgomery Clift in
Red River (1948).

WAYNE
FAMILY TIP

Get the most meat for
your money. Buy plump
meaty racks of ribs,
avoiding those with so
little meat you can see
shiny bones.

RED RIVER RIBS

This recipe is handy for entertaining because the initial
cooking can be done up to a day ahead. The ribs can then be
quickly finished on the grill or in the oven just before serving.

PROVISIONS

SAUCE

2 cups brown sugar

1 cup hot sauce

2 cups cider vinegar

½ cup molasses

RIBS

2½ lb. (about 2 racks) St. Louis-style ribs

½ cup olive oil

Sea salt

Freshly ground pepper

PREP

1. For sauce, combine ingredients in a heavy nonstick saucepan
and bring to a boil. Reduce heat to low, and simmer for about
an hour. Sauce should be thick and shiny. Refrigerate.

2. Preheat oven to 350 degrees F. Drizzle both sides of ribs with
oil and sprinkle with salt and pepper to taste. Place on baking
rack over rimmed baking sheet. Add 1½ cups water to baking
sheet and cover tightly with foil. Roast for 3 hours or until ribs
are tender. Meat should separate easily from bone.

3. Remove ribs from oven and let rest for at least 20 minutes.

4. Brush ribs on both sides with sauce and grill over medium
heat for 5 to 6 minutes per side.

SPICED PORK PATTIES
WITH SPRING GREENS

They might not win a beauty contest, but what these pork patties lack in looks they make up for in flavor and simplicity. Serve over a basic salad or split a few kaiser rolls to make sandwiches perfect for a backyard cookout.

PROVISIONS

1   lb. ground pork

1   tsp. ground coriander

1   tsp. cumin

½   tsp. cinnamon

¼   tsp. nutmeg

1   large egg, beaten

½   onion, finely chopped

¼   cup finely chopped fresh parsley

2   cloves garlic, chopped and divided

1½   tsp. salt

1   cup plain whole-milk yogurt

1½   tsp. lemon juice

10   cups mixed salad greens

PREP

1. Heat grill to medium. In bowl, combine pork, coriander, cumin, cinnamon, nutmeg, egg, onion, parsley, 1 garlic clove and 1 tsp. salt. Mix thoroughly with your hands. Form mixture into 1½-inch balls, then press into football shapes.

2. Grease up your grill grates. Grill patties, turning once, until cooked through or 8 to 10 minutes total.

3. In a small bowl, combine yogurt, lemon juice, ½ tsp. salt and remaining garlic. Divide salad greens among 4 serving plates. Top with patties and drizzle with yogurt sauce. Serve immediately.

John Wayne in *Rio Grande* (1950).

WAYNE FAMILY TIP

Never use lighter fluid; petroleum doesn't taste too good, and that's the flavor your meat absorbs when you resort to the easy way out. If you need help jumpstarting your coals, try fire starters.

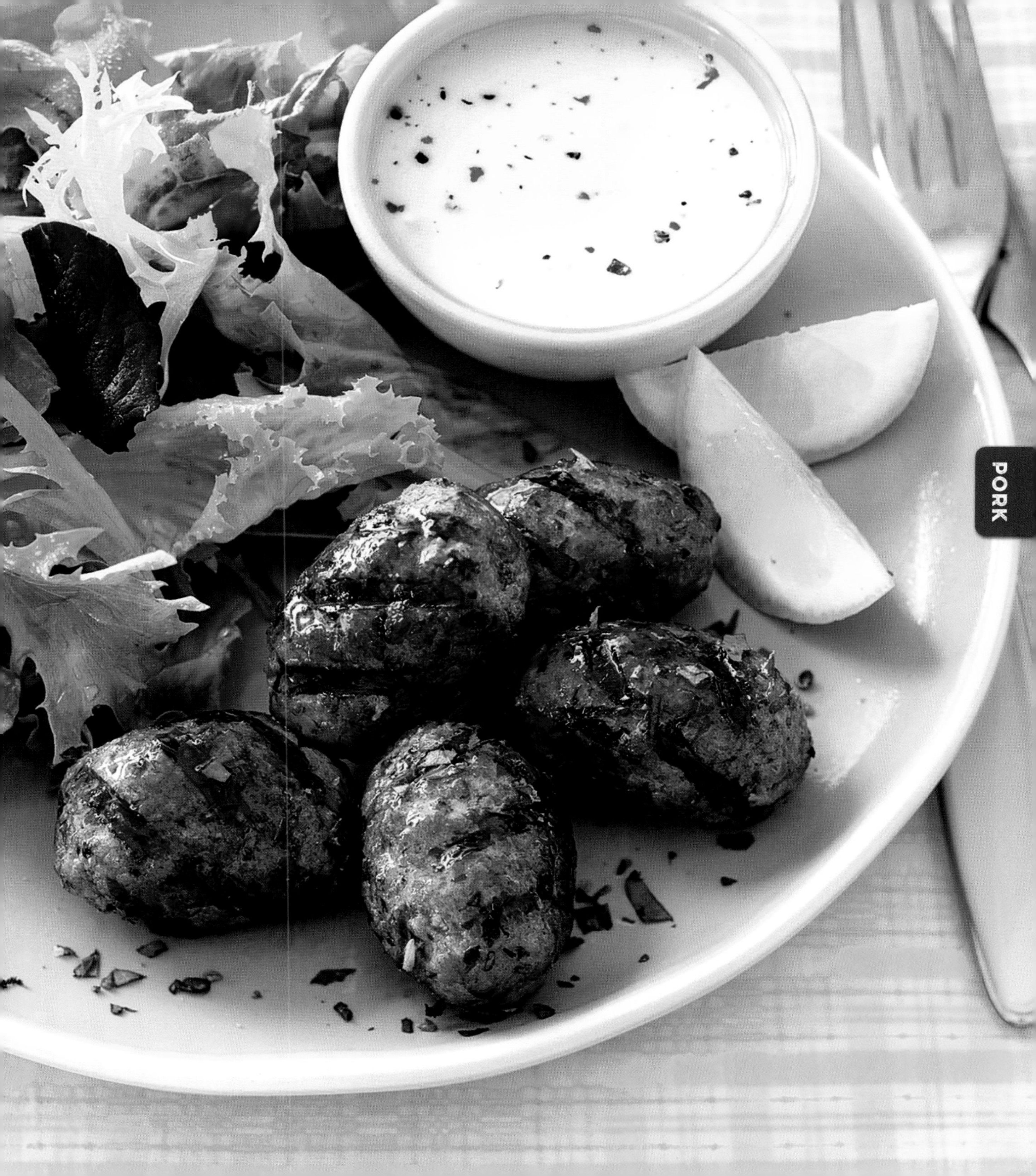

A MAGNIFICENT MEAL

John Wayne, Rita Hayworth and Miles Malleson have breakfast in *Circus World* (1964). In the United Kingdom, the film was released under the title *The Magnificent Showman*.

MUSTARD-MOLASSES PORK CHOPS

Served with a garlicky sauce composed of balsamic vinegar, molasses, mustard and fresh rosemary, then finished with a little crumbled Gorgonzola, these pork chops hit the spot any time of year.

PROVISIONS

⅔ cup balsamic vinegar

⅔ cup molasses

2 large cloves garlic, minced (about 1 Tbsp.)

1½ Tbsp. finely chopped fresh rosemary

½ cup Dijon mustard, divided

8 (¾-inch-thick) bone-in pork loin chops (about 4 lb. total)

2 Tbsp. olive oil

1 tsp. salt

1 tsp. pepper

1 Tbsp. butter

4 oz. crumbled Gorgonzola (about 1 cup)

PREP

1. Whisk vinegar, molasses, garlic, rosemary and ¼ cup mustard in a bowl. Divide marinade between 2 large zip-lock bags and add chops, flipping to coat. Seal and chill for 2 hours, flipping occasionally.

2. Heat grill to medium-high. Remove chops from marinade, shaking off excess. Set aside marinade. Brush chops with oil; sprinkle with salt and pepper.

3. Grill chops, covered, for 5 to 6 minutes on each side. Transfer chops to a plate and cover loosely with foil; let stand.

4. Whisk set-aside marinade and remaining ¼ cup mustard in a small saucepan. Bring to a boil over medium-high heat and cook, stirring frequently, for 4 minutes. (Sauce will be thick.) Remove from heat and whisk in butter until melted. Spoon sauce over chops, sprinkle with Gorgonzola and serve.

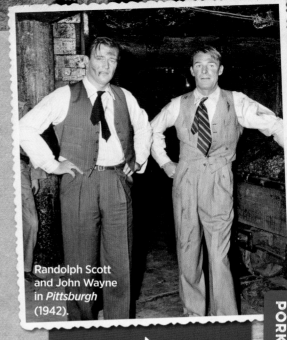

Randolph Scott and John Wayne in *Pittsburgh* (1942).

WAYNE FAMILY TIP

Plan ahead. Meat tastes best when left in its marinade overnight and put on the grill at room temperature. For flavor and simplicity's sake, do your prep the day before you grill.

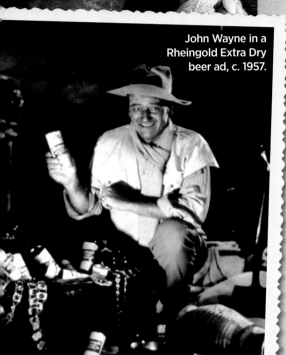

John Wayne in a Rheingold Extra Dry beer ad, c. 1957.

BEER-SOAKED SPICY RIBS

This rib dish takes a fair amount of planning, but all of the thinking ahead will pay off. Marinate your ribs two days ahead, grill them the day before, then reheat them on your grill at the party when you're ready to eat.

PROVISIONS

¾ cup harissa paste

3 Tbsp. fresh lemon juice

1 Tbsp. minced garlic

2 (1½-lb.) slabs baby back ribs

Kosher salt and freshly ground black pepper

2 (12-oz.) bottles beer, any type

PREP

1. In a small bowl, stir together harissa, lemon juice and garlic. Set aside.

2. Rinse ribs and pat dry. Use a dull butter knife to loosen the thin papery membrane that runs along underside, then pull it off with your fingers. Rub ribs generously on both sides with salt and pepper, then slather with homemade harissa rub. Wrap ribs in plastic wrap and marinate, refrigerated, for at least 8 and up to 24 hours.

3. Set up grill for medium indirect heat. Place ribs, bone side down, on the cooler part of the grill and close the lid. Cook, basting with beer on both sides every 10 minutes (keep ribs bone side down), for 40 to 50 minutes or until ribs are tender and cooked through and meat has shrunk back from ends of the bones. Try to keep harissa paste on the ribs while basting. Serve ribs hot.

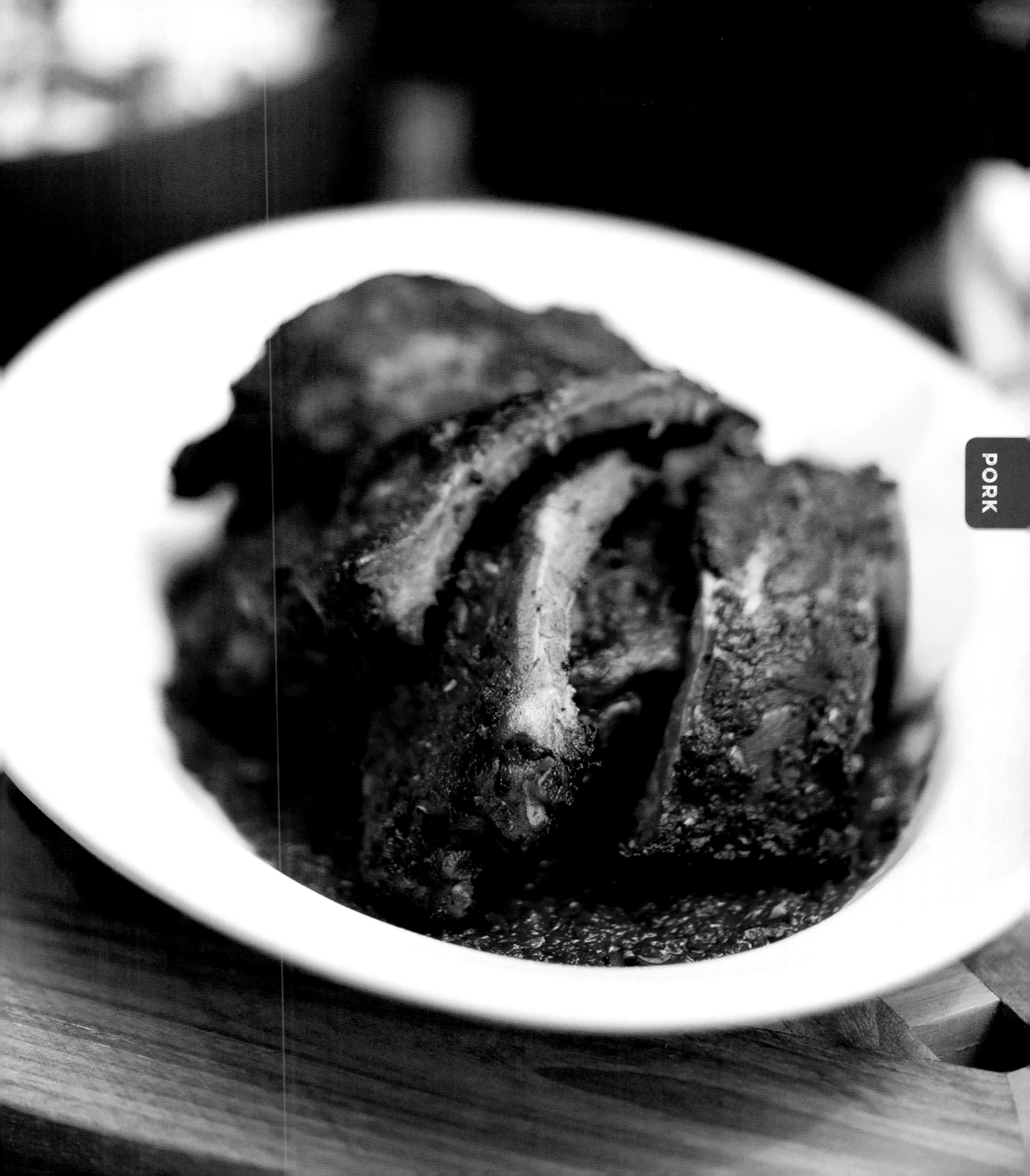

APRICOT PORK CHOPS

The beauty of pork chops is they're easy to make. The danger, of course, is overcooking them. Avoid making pork jerky on your grill by glazing these chops with an apricot sauce and keeping an eye on the heat and cook time.

PROVISIONS

⅔ **cup white wine**

⅓ **cup apricot preserves**

1 **tsp. finely chopped fresh thyme leaves**

Salt

4 **bone-in center-cut pork chops (about 3 lb.)**

1 **Tbsp. vegetable oil**

PREP

1. In a pot, mix wine, preserves, thyme and ½ tsp. salt. Bring to a boil over medium-high heat and cook until reduced by half. Cool.

2. Heat grill to medium-high. Rub chops with oil and sprinkle with salt. Grill for 10 minutes, turning once. Continue to cook, basting with glaze several times, 6 to 8 minutes longer. Let chops rest on a cutting board for 5 minutes before serving.

DID YOU KNOW?

California produces the most apricots of any state in America. Duke was a longtime—and easily recognizable—resident of the Golden State. "People might call out 'Hey Duke!' when he was running errands," Ethan says.

GRILLED WILD SALMON
PAGE 210

FISH

Duke loved the open water as much as he loved the Wild West.
Follow these recipes to cook up the catch of the day.

Fish Tacos

Glazed Salmon w/ Edamame Rice

Sunset Halibut

Upscale Scallops

Jamaican-Style Swordfish Steaks

Fresh Trout Filets

Grilled Wild Salmon

Grilled Shrimp w/ Tarator Sauce

Brown Sugar-Rubbed Salmon

Grilled Fish with Garden Salsa

FISH TACOS

These tacos are the perfect companion for a cool breeze and an evening on the water.

PROVISIONS

- 2 lb. white fish, such as tilapia, cod or halibut
- ½ tsp. kosher salt
- ¼ tsp. black pepper
- ½ cup sour cream
- ½ cup shredded coleslaw mix (shredded cabbage and carrots)
- 2 Tbsp. salsa
- 8 (6-inch) corn tortillas, for serving
- Lime wedges (optional)
- Chopped cilantro (optional)
- Avocado slices (optional)

PREP

1. Use a 4- or 6-quart slow cooker. Cube the fish and toss the cubes with salt and pepper. Place the fish pieces into the center of a length of foil or parchment paper. Fold over the edges and crimp to make a packet. Place the packet into your slow cooker insert.

2. Cover and cook on high for 2 hours or until the fish flakes easily with a fork. In a mixing bowl, combine the sour cream, coleslaw mix and salsa. Spoon this sauce on top of the fish and serve in warmed corn tortillas with desired garnishes.

John Wayne relaxes in Hawaii.

WAYNE FAMILY TIP

Short on time? You can grill or pan-fry the fish instead.

GLAZED SALMON WITH EDAMAME RICE

There's nothing fishy going on here. Just a darn good dish that's light but filling.

PROVISIONS

SALMON

- ¼ cup soy sauce
- ¼ cup firmly packed brown sugar
- 1 tsp. sesame oil
- 4 (4-oz.) salmon fillets, skin removed
- 1 Tbsp. rice wine vinegar
- 2 scallions, finely sliced on the diagonal
- 1 tsp. sesame seeds

RICE

- 2 cups water
- ½ tsp. kosher salt
- 2 tsp. soy sauce
- 2 Tbsp. rice wine vinegar
- 2 tsp. sesame oil
- ½ tsp. sugar
- 1 cup brown rice
- 1 (2.25-oz.) bag freeze dried soybeans

PREP

SALMON

1. In a shallow baking dish, combine the soy sauce, brown sugar and sesame oil. Add the salmon fillets and let marinate for 3 minutes. Flip and let marinate on the other side.

2. Heat a large skillet over medium-high. Add the salmon fillets and cook for 2 minutes. Flip the salmon over and cook for another 2 to 4 minutes, depending on how done you like your salmon. Remove from pan and pour the marinade into the hot skillet. Add the rice vinegar and cook, stirring until the sauce reduces slightly, about 2 minutes. Pour the sauce over the salmon, garnish with the scallions and sesame seeds. Serve immediately.

RICE

1. Combine the water, salt, soy sauce, vinegar, sesame oil, sugar, rice and soy beans in a saucepan; stir to combine and bring to a boil. Cover the pan, reduce to a simmer and let simmer for 20 to 25 minutes or until all the water has evaporated. Fluff with a fork, cover and let sit for 5 minutes.

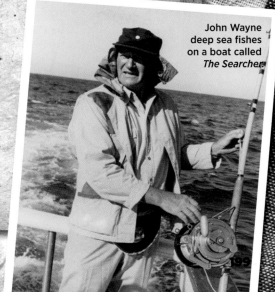

John Wayne deep sea fishes on a boat called *The Searcher.*

SUNSET HALIBUT
WITH FRESH MANGO SALSA

This sweet and tangy dish is the perfect meal for a warm summer night. The colorful mango salsa is fantastic with halibut but works well with other types of fish, too. Feel free to add extra heat with a teaspoon of cayenne.

PROVISIONS

- 2 cups plum tomatoes, seeded and diced
- 1½ cups peeled, diced ripe mango
- ½ cup diced onion
- ½ cup chopped fresh cilantro
- 2 Tbsp. fresh lime juice
- 1 Tbsp. cider vinegar
- 1 tsp. sugar
- 1 tsp. salt, divided
- 1 tsp. black pepper, divided
- 2 cloves garlic, minced
- 4 (6-oz.) halibut fillets
- 1 Tbsp. olive oil
- 1 tsp. cayenne, optional

PREP

1. To make the salsa, combine first seven ingredients and stir in ½ tsp. salt, ½ tsp. pepper and garlic.

2. Rub halibut with oil and dust with ½ tsp. salt and ½ tsp. pepper. Place fish on grill rack and grill 3 minutes on each side or until fish flakes with a fork.

3. Serve with mango salsa. There's nothing wrong with making a double batch of the salsa and serving it up with some chips—people are gonna want more.

DID YOU KNOW?

The mango is a major Peruvian export. Another dynamite export from Peru? Duke's wife, Pilar. He met her in Peru in 1953, while scouting locations for *The Alamo*.

John Wayne and his wife Pilar at their wedding in Hawaii, c. 1954.

FISH

John Wayne dons some dapper attire.

UPSCALE SCALLOPS
WITH TOMATO SAUCE AND SHORT PASTA

Scallops are high in protein and class, and they rate high on the flavor scale as well. This refreshing, easy-to-make dish tastes especially great at the height of summer when tomatoes are at their peak.

PROVISIONS

1 large tomato, seeded and chopped

½ cup chopped green onions

1 (⅔-oz.) package fresh mint leaves, chopped

⅓ cup orange juice

⅓ cup olive oil

¼ tsp. salt

¼ tsp. freshly ground black pepper

3 lb. sea scallops

2 cups hot cooked orzo (short pasta)

Salt and pepper to taste

PREP

1. Combine first seven ingredients in a bowl. Cover and chill for 2 hours.

2. Drain and reserve juice from the tomato mixture; set mixture and juice aside.

3. Thread scallops evenly onto skewers. Shake on salt and pepper, then brush scallops with the rest of the juice.

4. Grill scallops with lid on over medium-high heat for 3 to 4 minutes on each side or until scallops are opaque.

5. Serve over cooked orzo and top with the tomato sauce.

JAMAICAN-STYLE SWORDFISH STEAKS

Jamaican dishes are influenced by the cuisine of many cultures, including Mexican, West Indian and African. A unique blend of seasonings make these swordfish steaks anything but ordinary.

PROVISIONS

- ¾ cup plain yogurt
- 1 Tbsp. Jamaican jerk seasoning
- 1 Tbsp. fresh lemon juice
- 1 tsp. garlic powder
- 1 tsp. ground cumin
- 1 tsp. chili powder
- ½ tsp. ground cinnamon
- ½ tsp. ground ginger
- 4 (6-oz.) swordfish steaks (about ¾-inch thick)

PREP

1. Combine the first eight ingredients in a large bag. Add fish, flipping to coat. Cover and refrigerate for 1 hour, flipping the bag occasionally.

2. Prepare grill.

3. Place fish on grill rack coated with olive oil; grill for 4 minutes on each side or until fish flakes easily when tested with a fork or to desired degree of doneness.

John Wayne (far right), his son Patrick (center) and friends pose with the catch of the day.

FISH

DID YOU KNOW?

Duke loved sport fishing in the Gulf of California. The 62,000-square-mile span between northwestern Mexico and the Baja California Peninsula is a swordfish haven.

GRABBING A BITE BETWEEN TAKES
Clockwise from top left: Victor McLaglen, George O'Brien, Henry Fonda, Pedro Armendáriz, John Wayne, John Ford, Dick Foran (sideburns) and John Agar have dinner on the set of *Fort Apache* (1948).

FRESH TROUT FILLETS
TOPPED WITH CITRUS CRUNCH

Rainbow trout is one of the most sustainably raised fish, and they thrive in the Wild West of the Rockies. Because it's dense and oily, the fish is less likely to stick to the grill than others, so after you eat, it's easier to clean your setup.

PROVISIONS

- 2 Tbsp. pine nuts
- ¼ cup extra-virgin olive oil, divided
- ½ cup panko crumbs (Japanese bread crumbs)
- 2 oil-packed anchovy fillets, minced
- 1 Tbsp. minced garlic (3 medium cloves)
- ¾ tsp. salt, divided
- 2 tsp. very finely shredded lemon zest
- 1 Tbsp. finely chopped flat-leaf parsley leaves
- 2 medium heads radicchio
- 4 (½-inch thick) skin-on trout fillets
- 1 Tbsp. lemon juice
- Freshly ground black pepper

PREP

1. Toast pine nuts in a wide (not nonstick) frying pan over medium heat until lightly toasted or about 3 minutes. Pour into a medium bowl and set to the side.

2. In the same pan, heat 1 Tbsp. olive oil over medium heat until it's warm, then add panko. Toast the panko, stirring occasionally, for about 5 minutes or until it darkens up. Add the anchovies and garlic; stir to combine well.

3. Add the panko mixture to pine nuts. Stir in ¼ tsp. salt, lemon zest and parsley and set aside.

4. Preheat grill. Cut each radicchio head in half, then cut each half into thirds; brush cut sides with olive oil. Place wedges onto metal skewers, three per skewer. Grill the radicchio (close the lid if you're cooking over gas) for 2 minutes, then turn skewers to grill opposite side for about 2 minutes. Remove radicchio from skewers and chop roughly. Toss with remaining lemon juice and ½ tsp. salt.

5. Brush fish on both sides with olive oil and grill, skin side down, for 3 to 4 minutes (close that lid again, gas grillers) or until fillets look opaque. Using two spatulas, gently turn fish over and cook for 1 minute. Carefully remove from the grill and transfer the fillets to plates.

6. Stir remaining 3 Tbsp. olive oil into panko mixture and spoon over the flesh side of fish. Season with salt, pepper and a few drops of lemon juice to taste. Serve with a side of grilled radicchio.

WAYNE FAMILY TIP

To keep delicate pieces of trout from breaking apart on your spatula, grill it on a bed of lemon slices. It'll add a zip of flavor and will keep you from cursing at your dinner when it crumbles into your charcoal.

GRILLED WILD SALMON
WITH MUSHROOM SAUCE AND ROASTED BEETS

The savory mushroom sauce matched with the rustic flavor of beets kick this salmon dish up a notch. If you're feeling fancy, feel free to serve the entire meal over a bed of arugula.

Great Alaskan Wild

Although John Wayne's 1960 film North to Alaska is set in the 49th state, most of it was filmed in California—the cabin is near a creek later used in True Grit (1969). Alaska is a major source of wild salmon, and more than half the nation's seafood is harvested there.

PROVISIONS

SALMON

18   baby red beets

18   baby yellow beets

    Olive oil

1   lb. wild Pacific salmon

    Salt

    Freshly ground black pepper

½   lb. arugula (optional)

SAUCE

3   cups chicken broth

2   Tbsp. chopped dried porcini or shiitake mushrooms

2   tsp. chopped fresh rosemary

1   large garlic clove, chopped

⅓   cup balsamic vinegar

1   Tbsp. butter

    Salt

    Freshly ground black pepper

PREP

1. To make the sauce, put the first four ingredients in a saucepan over high heat and bring to a boil. Cook over high heat for 15 to 20 minutes or until reduced by half. Stir in vinegar. Cook for 10 minutes or until mixture has reduced to about ½ cup and has the consistency of a light sauce.

2. Remove from heat, strain sauce through a fine-mesh strainer and return to pan. Whisk in butter. Season to taste with salt and pepper.

3. To cook beets, scrub them thoroughly and remove greens. Drizzle lightly with olive oil and place in a roasting pan. Bake, covered with foil, at 400 degrees F for 30 minutes or until tender. Rub the skins off beets with a towel and slice.

4. For salmon, remove any bones, then brush with olive oil and season lightly with salt and pepper. Grill salmon over medium-hot coals on both sides until medium rare (translucent in the center). Spread some sauce on the plates and top with beet slices. Cut salmon into servings and place on plates or on a bed of greens.

GRILLED SHRIMP
WITH TARATOR SAUCE

Let's face it: Shrimp are great whether they're boiled, fried or grilled. But grilling them adds a rich flavor you won't get through other cooking methods and is about as simple as tying your shoes. The toughest thing about this dish is the tarator sauce, which you'll find worth the effort as it cools things down on even the hottest summer day.

PROVISIONS

SHRIMP

2¾ lb. (about 50) fresh large shrimp, peeled and deveined

½ cup extra virgin olive oil

2 large garlic cloves, thinly sliced

4 fresh rosemary sprigs

SAUCE

2 cups pine nuts

3 slices firm-textured white bread with crust removed, torn into 1-inch pieces

½ cup fresh lemon juice

2 cloves garlic

¾ tsp. salt

½ tsp. freshly ground pepper

WAYNE FAMILY TIP

When you're grilling small items like shrimp, use two skewers to prevent the pieces from rotating or falling off into the grill.

PREP

1. Place sauce ingredients in a food processor with ⅓ cup water and process for 30 seconds. Scrape sides of bowl and process 30 more seconds or until smooth. Cover and chill until ready to serve.

2. Place first three shrimp ingredients in a large shallow baking dish and toss well. Squeeze the rosemary sprigs to release flavor, then add to shrimp mixture. Cover and refrigerate for 3 to 4 hours.

3. Thread 5 shrimp on each of the 10 long skewers, leaving space between shrimp. Grill with lid on over high heat for 1½ minutes on each side or to desired degree of doneness.

4. Serve hot or at room temperature with tarator sauce.

John Wayne enjoys a day of fishing.

BROWN SUGAR-RUBBED SALMON

Brown sugar isn't just for baking. When grilled, the brown sugar-paprika rub turns slightly crusty and caramelizes, giving the salmon a flavor and texture that'll have you wishing you'd made twice as much.

PROVISIONS

1 cup firmly packed brown sugar

½ cup paprika

¼ cup kosher salt

2 Tbsp. dried thyme

1 (2-lb.) salmon fillet, cut into portions

PREP

1. Combine first four ingredients. Coat both sides of the salmon with the rub; let sit 10 minutes.

2. Grill salmon over medium-high heat 3 to 4 minutes on each side or to desired degree of doneness. If you want, garnish with thyme.

WAYNE FAMILY TIP

Be careful when removing the salmon's pin bones. Ripping them upward and outward tears the fish's flesh. Instead, use a set of tweezers to pull the bones out in their natural direction.

GRILLED FISH
WITH GARDEN SALSA

If you're looking for a simple way to spice up just about any grilled white fish, top it with this homemade salsa that's brimming with fresh vegetables and a touch of heat, courtesy of a fresh jalapeño pepper. This versatile dish works with any type of mild, firm white fish fillets.

PROVISIONS

1 ½ tsp. ground cumin, divided

½ tsp. salt, divided

1 tsp. grated lime rind

2 Tbsp. fresh lime juice

1 Tbsp. olive oil

1 cucumber, chopped

1 cup grape tomatoes, halved

1 green onion, thinly sliced

1 jalapeño pepper, seeded and minced

1 Tbsp. chopped fresh mint

1 lb. mild, firm white fish fillets

PREP

1. Combine 1 tsp. cumin, ¼ tsp. salt, lime rind, lime juice and olive oil in a medium bowl. Add cucumber, tomatoes, green onion, jalapeño and mint; set salsa aside.

2. Toss remaining ½ tsp. cumin and ¼ tsp. salt over fish. Grill over medium-high heat for 7 minutes or until tender.

3. Top with salsa and serve. You can make the salsa any time and keep it in the fridge 'til company comes over and you're ready to grill, but use it within the week.

John Wayne holds the day's catch aboard the *Wild Goose*.

WAYNE FAMILY TIP

To create less mess when you grill fish, use aluminum foil instead of a grill pan. That way, come clean-up time, instead of scraping burnt fish skin off your pan while debating whether to throw it away, you can just ball up the foil and dump it in the trash.

COWBOY BURGERS
PAGE 230

BURGERS

Whether you're cooking for a few friends or a family reunion, burgers are fast, flavorful crowd-pleasers.

All-American Burger

BLT Burger

Duke's Burgers

War Wagon Burgers

Cowboy Burgers

South of the Border Burgers

Prospector's Pork Burgers

Wild West Chicken
and Cheddar Burgers

Southwestern Turkey Burgers

Spicy Sausage Cheese Burgers

Big Game Ham-and-Swiss-Stuffed
Burgers

ALL-AMERICAN BURGER

This isn't just the burger you need. It's the one you deserve. Eat up!

PROVISIONS

- ½ lb. ground chuck
- Kosher or fine sea salt, to taste
- Pepper, to taste
- 2 Tbsp. vegetable oil
- 4 slices American cheese
- 4 hamburger buns
- Ketchup, to serve
- Mustard, to serve
- Lettuce, to serve
- Tomatoes, to serve
- Dill chip pickles, to serve
- Onion, to serve

PREP

1. Place a cast-iron skillet in the oven and heat to 500 degrees F.

2. Divide the ground chuck into 4 equal-sized portions. Loosely form each portion into a patty ¾-in. thick. Make a deep impression in the center of each patty and season generously with salt and pepper on both sides. Place in the refrigerator while the oven heats up.

3. When the oven reaches 500 degrees F, carefully remove the skillet and place on the stove over medium-high heat and turn off the oven.

4. Add the oil to the pan and heat until it shimmers. Add the patties and cook until the burgers are golden brown and slightly charred, about 3 minutes. Flip the burgers and cook for 3 minutes. Add a slice of cheese to each burger, place a lid or another skillet over the pan, and cook for another minute or two or until the bottom of the burgers are golden brown and slightly charred and the cheese has melted.

5. Serve on buns with fixings on the side so each diner can build their perfect burger.

John Wayne in *Arizona* (1931).

BLT BURGER

Sometimes, it's the simple things in life that give us the most pleasure.
And it doesn't get simpler than bacon, lettuce, tomato and beef.

PROVISIONS

SAUCE

- ¾ cup mayonnaise
- ¼ cup ketchup
- 2 Tbsp. sweet chili sauce
- 2 Tbsp. pickle relish
- 2 Tbsp. very finely minced white onion
- 1 Tbsp. Worcestershire sauce

BURGERS

- 6 slices thick cut bacon, cut in half crosswise
- 2 lb. ground chuck
  Kosher or fine sea salt, to taste
  Pepper, to taste
- 6 Kaiser rolls or hamburger buns
  Lettuce leaves
  Thick slices of tomato

PREP

SAUCE

1. Combine all ingredients in a mixing bowl and mix well. Cover with plastic wrap and refrigerate until serving time.

BURGERS

1. Place the bacon in a cold cast-iron skillet, turn the heat to medium, and cook the bacon until crispy, turning occasionally. Let drain on paper towels.

2. Divide the ground chuck into 6 equal-sized portions. Loosely form each portion into a patty ¾-in. thick. Make a deep impression in the center of each patty and season generously with salt and pepper on both sides.

3. Remove all but 3 Tbsp. of bacon fat and turn the heat to medium-high. Add the patties and cook until the burgers are golden brown and slightly charred, about 3 minutes. Flip the burgers and cook for 4 minutes (for medium-rare) or until golden brown and slightly charred.

4. Spread sauce on both sides of the burger buns, put lettuce and tomato on the bottom bun, top with burger patty and bacon.

DID YOU KNOW?

The word "hatari" means "danger" in Swahili, but the film's actors managed to make it through the shoot without suffering serious harm, despite working with live animals.

John Wayne and a cheetah in *Hatari!* (1962).

DUKE'S BURGERS

Like John Wayne, these burgers are quintessentially American and guaranteed to be a favorite with your family.

PROVISIONS

- 1½ lb. ground chuck
- ½ lb. ground sirloin
- 1 tsp. kosher salt
- ¾ tsp. black pepper
- 3 Tbsp. melted butter or extra-virgin olive oil
- 6 hamburger buns

PREP

1. Preheat the grill to medium-high.

2. Combine the ground chuck, sirloin, salt and pepper. Gently mix with your hands, being careful not to over-mix. Divide the meat into 6 equal portions. Shape into flat, uniform patties. Using your thumb, make an indentation in the center of each patty.

3. Cook 5 minutes per side for medium burgers. Before taking the burgers off the grill, brush them with melted butter or olive oil.

4. Toast the buns on the grill if desired and serve with the burgers.

Duke on the set of *Big Jim McLain* (1952).

BURGERS

WAYNE FAMILY TIP

You can flavor these burgers any way you wish! Add in garlic powder, soy sauce (if using, skip the salt) or mix in grated cheese for a fun twist.

WAR WAGON BURGERS

These ground rounds will help you fuel up before you hit the trails.

PROVISIONS

- 1 (8-count) pkg. refrigerated ready-to-bake jumbo biscuits
- 2 Tbsp. melted butter
- 1 cup canned chili
- 3 lb. ground chuck (80 percent lean)
- Vegetable oil, for patties
- Kosher or fine sea salt, to taste
- Pepper, to taste
- 1 cup shredded cheddar cheese
- ½ cup chopped onion

PREP

1. Bake the biscuits according to the package directions. Cut in half, brush the cut sides with melted butter and keep warm.

2. Prepare the grill for direct heat and heat to medium-high. Place the chili in a saucepan and heat on the grill or on the stove. Keep warm.

3. Divide the meat into 8 equal portions. Form each portion loosely into a ¾-inch-thick patty and make a depression in the center of each patty with your thumb. Brush the patties with oil and season generously with salt and pepper.

4. Grill the burgers 3 to 4 minutes per side for medium rare. Serve the burgers on the biscuits topped with chili, grated cheese and chopped onion.

Kirk Douglas and John Wayne in *The War Wagon* (1967).

COWBOY BURGERS

Like the Ringo Kid or Quirt Evans, these burgers
are an American classic you'll keep revisiting again and again.

PROVISIONS

- 1½ lb. ground chuck (80-percent lean)
-    Vegetable oil, for patties
-    Kosher or fine sea salt, to taste
-    Freshly ground black pepper, to taste
- ¾ cup barbecue sauce
- 6 slices cheddar or American cheese
- 6 hamburger buns
- 1 (6-oz.) container French fried onions

PREP

1. Prepare the grill for direct heat and heat to medium-high.

2. Divide ground chuck into 6 equal portions. Form each portion into patties and make a depression in the center of each patty with your thumb. Brush the patties with oil and season with salt and pepper.

3. Grill the burgers for 4 minutes with lid closed. Brush with barbecue sauce, flip, brush the top of the burger with more sauce, and grill for another 3 minutes. Top each patty with a slice of cheese, close the lid and grill for another minute.

4. Brush both sides of the buns with barbecue sauce. Top the burgers with French fried onions.

John Wayne in
The Cowboys
(1972).

SOUTH OF THE BORDER BURGERS

Like many of Duke's characters, these spicy burgers reflect the rich
cultural melting pot of the West.

PROVISIONS

- 1½ lb. ground chuck (80 percent lean)
- 1 (10-oz.) can tomatoes and chilies, drained
- Vegetable oil, for patties
- Kosher or fine sea salt, to taste
- Pepper, to taste
- 6 slices pepper jack cheese
- 6 hamburger buns
- 2 ripe avocados
- 1 lime, juiced
- Salsa
- 6 hamburger buns

PREP

1. Prepare the grill for direct heat and heat
to medium-high.

2. In a large mixing bowl, combine the
meat with the drained tomatoes and
chilies. Divide into 6 equal portions.
Form each portion into patties and make
a depression in the center of each patty
with your thumb. Brush the patties with
oil and season with salt and pepper.

3. Grill the burgers for 4 minutes with
the lid closed. Flip and grill for another
3 minutes. Top each patty with a slice of
cheese, close the lid and grill for another
minute. Toast the buns lightly on the grill.

4. Mash the avocados with lime juice and
salt and pepper to taste.

5. Serve the burgers on buns topped with
the mashed avocado
and salsa.

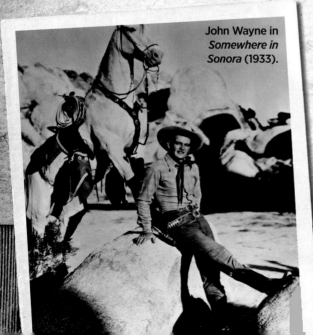

John Wayne in
*Somewhere in
Sonora* (1933).

DID YOU KNOW?

Mexico was one of John Wayne's
favorite vacation destinations.
He even owned part of a luxury
hotel in Acapulco, Hotel Los
Flamingos, where he could
kick back in style.

PROSPECTOR'S PORK BURGERS

If you've been looking for a burger with the perfect touch of sweetness, you've hit the motherlode.

PROVISIONS

QUICK APPLE CHUTNEY

- 1 Tbsp. butter
- 2 apples, cored and chopped
- 3 Tbsp. brown sugar
- 2 Tbsp. apple cider vinegar
- ½ tsp. dried ginger

PORK BURGERS

- 1 lb. ground pork
- 1 tsp. garlic powder
- 1 tsp. kosher or fine sea salt
- ½ tsp. dried sage
- ½ tsp. pepper
-   Vegetable oil, for grill
- 4 biscuits or hamburger buns

PREP

CHUTNEY

1. In a medium skillet, melt the butter over medium heat. Add the apples, brown sugar, vinegar and ginger and stir to combine. Cook the apples, uncovered, stirring occasionally until tender, about 8 minutes. Raise the heat to high and cook, stirring, for another minute or two until all the liquid has evaporated. Let cool.

BURGERS

1. Prepare grill for direct heat and preheat to medium-high.

2. Combine the pork, garlic powder, salt, sage and pepper in a medium mixing bowl. Divide the mixture into 4 equal portions, shape into patties and make a deep impression with your thumb in the center of each patty. Brush the grill grates with oil and grill the patties with the lid closed 4 to 5 minutes per side.

3. Place some of the apple chutney on the bottom half of each biscuit or bun, top with a pork burger, a large dollop of chutney and finally the top half of the biscuit or bun.

John Wayne in *North to Alaska* (1960).

DID YOU KNOW?

In one scene from *North to Alaska*, John Wayne's character searches for a man in a bar while a version of a song called "North to Alaska" plays in the background.

THE FAMILY LEGACY LIVES ON

John Wayne poses with four generations of his family, including his mother (center), his children and grandchildren. Duke's mother would sometimes visit her son on film sets.

WILD WEST CHICKEN AND CHEDDAR BURGERS

The original burger is an American classic, but this daring dish gives it a run for its money.

PROVISIONS

- 1½ lb. ground chicken
- Vegetable oil, for patties
- Kosher or fine sea salt, to taste
- Pepper, to taste
- 4 slices cheddar cheese
- 4 hamburger buns
- Mayonnaise
- 4 lettuce leaves
- 8 slices tomatoes
- 4 slices onion

PREP

1. Prepare the grill for direct heat and heat to medium-high.

2. Divide the chicken into 4 equal-sized portions. Form each portion into patties and make a depression in the center of each patty with your thumb. Brush the patties with oil and season with salt and pepper.

3. Grill the burgers for 4 minutes with the lid closed. Flip and cook another 3 minutes, top each patty with a slice of cheese, close the lid and grill for another minute or until the burgers are cooked through and the cheese melts.

4. Lightly grill the hamburger buns. Spread some mayonnaise on each side of the bun. Serve the burgers on the buns with lettuce, tomato and onion.

DID YOU KNOW?

John Wayne became well-acquainted with Monument Valley and eventually began collecting Hopi kachina dolls, which are traditionally used as learning tools within the Hopi Native American tribe that populated the region.

Frank McGrath and John Wayne in *She Wore a Yellow Ribbon* (1949).

SOUTHWESTERN TURKEY BURGERS

You'd be a turkey not to gobble down these burgers by the plateful.

PROVISIONS

- ½ cup mayonnaise
- 1 Tbsp. Sriracha sauce
- 1½ lb. ground turkey
- ½ cup grated cheddar cheese
- Vegetable oil, for patties
- Kosher or fine sea salt, to taste
- Pepper, to taste
- 4 hamburger buns
- 1 avocado, sliced

John Wayne in *The New Frontier* (1935).

PREP

1. Combine the mayonnaise and Sriracha sauce in a small bowl. Refrigerate, covered until ready to serve.

2. Prepare the grill for direct heat and heat to medium-high.

3. Combine the turkey and cheese in a large mixing bowl. Divide into 4 equal-sized portions. Form each portion into patties and make a depression in the center of each patty with your thumb. Brush the patties with oil and season with salt and pepper.

4. Grill the burgers for 4 minutes with the lid closed. Flip and cook another 4 minutes or until the burgers are cooked through.

5. Lightly grill the hamburger buns. Spread some spicy mayonnaise on each side of the bun. Serve the burgers on the buns with avocado slices.

WAYNE FAMILY TIP

To ensure you're buying ripe avocados, give them a little squeeze. If it feels like a stone, it needs a few days to ripen. If it almost explodes, it's too far gone. But if it gives just a little under pressure, take it to the checkout counter.

SPICY SAUSAGE CHEESE BURGERS

These burgers really pack a punch—and a kick.

PROVISIONS

PEPPER COMPOTE

- 1 Tbsp. olive oil
- 1 small white onion, finely diced
- ½ red bell pepper, seeded and finely chopped
- ½ green bell pepper, seeded and finely chopped
- ½ tsp. kosher or fine sea salt
- ¼ tsp. pepper

BURGERS

- 1 lb. loose breakfast or Italian sausage
- Vegetable oil, for patties
- 4 slices cheddar cheese
- 1 stick butter, at room temperature
- 2 garlic cloves, minced
- 4 hamburger rolls

PREP

PEPPER COMPOTE

1. In a medium skillet over medium-high, heat the oil. Add the onion, peppers, salt and pepper and cook, stirring occasionally, until the vegetables are soft and starting to brown, about 10 minutes. Reserve until serving time.

BURGERS

1. Prepare the grill for direct and indirect heat and preheat to medium.

Verna Hillie and John Wayne in *The Star Packer* (1934).

2. Divide the sausage into 4 equal portions, shape into patties, and make a deep impression with your thumb in the center of each patty. Brush the patties with oil, and grill over direct heat with the lid closed 4 to 5 minutes per side. Place a slice of cheese on top of each burger 1 minute before done and cook with lid closed until the cheese starts to melt, about 1 minute.

3. Position top oven rack 6 in. from top and preheat the broiler to high.

4. Combine the butter and garlic. Spread over both halves of the hamburger buns. Place the buns on a baking sheet, cut side up and broil until toasted, about 1 to 2 minutes.

5. Serve the sausage burgers on the garlic toasted buns topped with pepper compote.

WAYNE FAMILY TIP

If you want even more kick with each bite of these burgers, spicy brown mustard is a complementary condiment.

KICKING BACK IN STYLE
John Wayne enjoys a rare repose from his hectic schedule. The icon enjoyed activities such as fishing, hunting, mining and playing chess and cards in his free time between films.

BIG GAME HAM-AND SWISS-STUFFED BURGERS

When you need a big meal before the big game, the only thing better than meat is more meat. This ham- and swiss-stuffed burger is a tasty alternative to the classic patty, and it's just as simple to make.

DID YOU KNOW?

For a time, John Wayne sponsored and coached the John Wayne Giants little league team, teaching L.A. boys to enjoy the great American pastime.

PROVISIONS

- 1 Tbsp. dried parsley
- 1 Tbsp. Worcestershire sauce
- ¼ tsp. salt
- ¼ tsp. garlic powder
- ¼ tsp. freshly ground black pepper
- 1 lb. ground round
- ½ cup (2 oz.) shredded Swiss cheese
- 2 oz. smoked deli ham, thinly sliced
- 8 (1-oz.) slices sourdough bread
- 4 curly leaf lettuce leaves
- 8 (¼-inch-thick) slices red onion
- 8 (¼-inch-thick) slices tomato

PREP

1. Prepare grill, setting it to high heat and greasing its grates.

2. Combine first six ingredients. Divide mixture into eight equal portions, forming each into a 5-inch oval patty. These are going to be the tops and bottoms of your burgers. Take four of the patties and top them with 2 Tbsp. cheese and ½ oz. ham, leaving a ½-inch border around the outer edges; top with remaining patties. Press edges together to seal.

3. Put patties on your grill rack. Grill for 3 minutes on each side or until done. Place bread on grill rack and grill for 1 minute on each side or until toasted. Top each of four bread slices with one lettuce leaf, two onion slices, one patty, two tomato slices and one bread slice.

**GREEN BERET
GREEN BEANS
& BACON**

PAGE 292

SIDES

Every star needs a sidekick, and these dishes are sure to complement your main attraction.

Bacony Baked Beans

Maple Bacon Brussels Sprouts

Blistered Green Beans
and Tomatoes

Skillet Hasselback Potatoes

Skillet-Style Mexican
Street Corn

All-American Onion Rings

Cheesy Breadsticks

South-of-the-Border
Mexican Rice

Roasted Potatoes

Heartland Creamed Corn

Duke's Mac and Cheese

Supreme Pasta Salad

Scalloped Cheddar Potatoes

Grilled Garden Medley

Backyard Coleslaw

Angel and the
Badman Biscuits

Old-School Creamed Spinach

Sweet Peach Salad

3 Godfathers Garlic Potatoes

Green Beret
Green Beans and Bacon

New Frontier Vegetable Salad

Star Packer Potato Salad

BACONY BAKED BEANS

How do you make a cowboy classic even better? Just add bacon.

PROVISIONS

- 1 lb. dried white beans
- 6 slices thick cut bacon, chopped
- 1 large white or yellow onion, diced
- 1 jalapeño pepper, seeded, deveined and minced
- 1 cup barbecue sauce
- ½ cup light brown sugar, packed
- ¼ cup ketchup
- ¼ cup apple cider vinegar
- 1 tsp. dry mustard

PREP

1. Place the beans in a large bowl, cover with water and soak overnight. Drain and rinse the beans, place in a cast-iron Dutch oven, cover with fresh water, bring to a boil, reduce the heat, cover the pot and simmer for 2 hours. Drain the beans.

2. Preheat oven to 325 degrees F.

3. Rinse and dry the Dutch oven, put back on the stove over medium heat, add the bacon and cook, stirring occasionally, until cooked through but not crispy. Add the onion and cook, stirring occasionally, until tender, about 5 minutes. Add the jalapeño pepper and cook, stirring, for one minute. Add the beans back to the pot along with the rest of the ingredients. Cook for 2 to 3 minutes, stirring.

4. Put the lid on the Dutch oven and bake for 2 hours or until the sauce is the consistency of syrup. Let sit for a few minutes before serving, if desired.

John Wayne in *Red River* (1948).

SIDES

DID YOU KNOW?

John Wayne and legendary director Howard Hawks made five films together, starting with *Red River* in 1948.

MAPLE BACON BRUSSELS SPROUTS

Hold it right there, pilgrim! You've just discovered the perfect side for any occasion.

PROVISIONS

- **4 slices thick cut bacon**
- **2 Tbsp. butter**
- **1 lb. Brussels sprouts, trimmed and cut in half**
- **3 Tbsp. maple syrup**
- **Kosher or fine sea salt, to taste**
- **Pepper, to taste**

PREP

1. Slice the bacon widthwise into ¼-in. strips. Place in a cold cast-iron skillet, turn the heat to medium and cook, stirring occasionally, until crisp. Remove from the skillet with a slotted spoon and drain on paper towels.

2. Add the butter to the pan, let the butter melt, then add the Brussels sprouts. Cook, stirring occasionally, until fork tender. Add the maple syrup and bacon, and cook for another 30 to 60 seconds, stirring to coat the Brussels sprouts with the maple syrup. Season to taste with salt and pepper.

Jeffrey Hunter, John Wayne and Ward Bond in *The Searchers* (1956).

WAYNE FAMILY TIP

It's important to size up your sprouts to pick the ones best suited to your tastes. Bigger sprouts tend to taste bitter, while smaller sprouts have a subtle sweetness.

BLISTERED GREEN BEANS & TOMATOES

One helping of this side dish, and you'll never
hear 'em complain about eating their vegetables again.

PROVISIONS

- 1 Tbsp. olive oil
- 2 Tbsp. butter
- 1 lb. green beans, trimmed
- 1½ cups cherry or grape tomatoes, halved
- 2 garlic cloves, minced
- 1 Tbsp. balsamic vinegar

  Kosher or fine sea salt, to taste

  Pepper, to taste

PREP

1. Heat a cast-iron skillet over medium-high for 3 minutes. Add the oil and butter and, when the butter has melted, the green beans, tomatoes and garlic. Let sit for 90 seconds, undisturbed. Toss and cook for another 2 to 3 minutes or until the beans are crisp tender and the tomatoes start breaking down. Add the vinegar, toss to coat, season to taste with salt and pepper and serve.

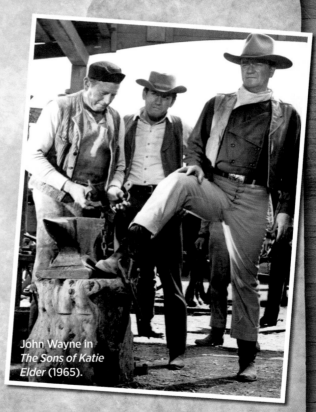

John Wayne in
*The Sons of Katie
Elder* (1965).

SKILLET HASSELBACK POTATOES

This no-frills potato dish is guaranteed to become an instant favorite from your first bite.

PROVISIONS

- 6 medium Idaho potatoes
- ½ cup butter, melted
- ¼ cup olive oil
- 6 Tbsp. chopped chives
- 2 tsp. kosher or fine sea salt
- 1 tsp. pepper

PREP

1. Preheat oven to 450 degrees F.

2. Scrub the potatoes and slice them into thin slices, leaving the bottom ¼ in. uncut. Place the potatoes in a cast-iron skillet.

3. Combine the melted butter, olive oil, chives, salt and pepper. Brush the potatoes with the mixture, making sure to get it down in between the slices. Save a little bit of the butter mixture to brush on after the potatoes are done baking.

4. Bake for 1 hour or until tender. Brush with the reserved butter mixture and serve.

DID YOU KNOW?

Despite being a globe-trotting celebrity who could dine at the finest of establishments, Duke never strayed from his humble roots as a "meat and potatoes" guy.

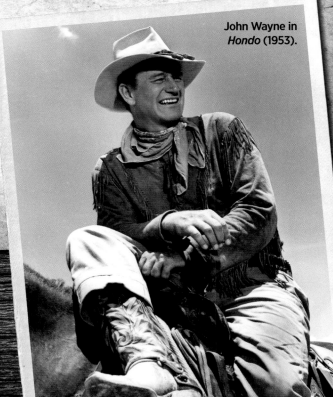

John Wayne in *Hondo* (1953).

SKILLET-STYLE MEXICAN STREET CORN

One spoonful of this flavorful side dish is like treating your tastebuds to a well-deserved fiesta.

PROVISIONS

- **1**   Tbsp. olive oil
- **4**   cups fresh or frozen (and thawed) corn kernels
- **1**   (10-oz.) can diced tomatoes and green chilies, drained
- **¾**   cup grated Cotija cheese, divided
- **½**   cup mayonnaise
-     Zest of 1 lime, finely grated
- **¼**   cup fresh cilantro leaves, coarsely chopped
-     Lime wedges, to serve

PREP

1. Heat the oil in a cast-iron skillet until it shimmers. Add the corn and spread into an even layer. Cook, stirring and smoothing back into an even layer occasionally, until the corn starts to brown, about 5 minutes.

2. Add the canned tomatoes and green chilies and cook, stirring, for 1 minute. Add ½ cup cheese, mayonnaise and lime zest, and cook for another minute, stirring. Stir in the cilantro leaves, top with the remaining cheese and serve with lime wedges.

John Wayne and his youngest son Ethan pose for a picture.

WAYNE FAMILY TIP

Want to add a little spice to your street corn? Use pepper jack cheese instead of Cotija and hang on to your hat!

ALL-AMERICAN ONION RINGS

The perfect snack to chow down on in the company of friends and family on a hot summer afternoon—or anytime.

PROVISIONS

- 2 large white onions
- 2½ tsp. kosher or fine sea salt
- 2 tsp. black pepper
- 2 cups buttermilk
- 1½ cups flour
- ¼ cup yellow cornmeal
- 1 qt. vegetable oil

PREP

1. Preheat oven to 200 degrees F.

2. Peel onions and slice them ½ to ¾ inch thick. Separate into rings.

3. In a bowl, add 1 tsp. of salt and 1 tsp. of pepper to the buttermilk. Drop the onion rings into the buttermilk mixture and let set for half an hour (can sit as long as a few hours). Mix the flour and cornmeal with 1 ½ tsp. of salt and 1 tsp. of pepper.

4. Heat the vegetable oil in a large pot or Dutch oven to 275 degrees F. Working in small batches, take some onion rings out of the buttermilk and dredge in the flour mixture, then carefully drop into the hot oil. Make sure you do not over crowd. Fry for about 2 minutes or until golden brown turning once during frying. Take onion rings out of the oil and put on the prepared baking sheet and sprinkle with some additional salt. Keep them warm in the oven while you fry the rest of the onion rings.

5. Serve hot.

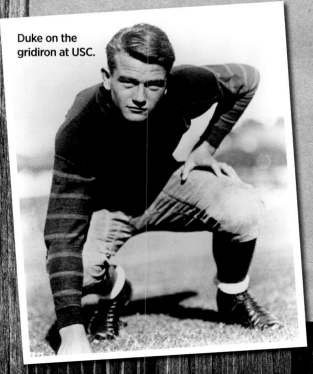

Duke on the gridiron at USC.

CHEESY BREADSTICKS

Duke loved classic Italian cuisine, and these pieces of culinary perfection
are another way to enjoy the tastes of the Old Country.

PROVISIONS

- 1 (7.5-oz.) box breadstick mix
- 1½ cups grated Parmesan cheese, divided
- 2 large eggs
- 2 Tbsp. olive oil, plus more for brushing the breadsticks
- ¼ cup water
- 8 oz. mozzarella or string cheese
- ½ cup pizza sauce

PREP

1. Preheat oven to 375 degrees F. Line a baking sheet with parchment paper or a silicone baking mat.

2. In a mixing bowl, combine the breadstick mix, 1 cup Parmesan, eggs, 2 Tbsp. olive oil and water. Mix until it just begins to form a dough; it is OK if the dough is crumbly. Dump the mixture out onto a clean work surface and knead until smooth.

3. Roll the dough into a rectangle 8 inches by 16 inches. Cut the dough into 2- by 8-inch strips.

4. Cut the cheese into thin strips and divide among the dough, laying on top. Brush some water on the edges of the dough and seal. Roll the dough gently to make round logs. Place the breadsticks on the prepared baking sheet. Brush the tops of the breadsticks with olive oil and sprinkle with the remaining Parmesan cheese. Bake for 20 to 25 minutes or until golden brown.

5. Serve warm with pizza sauce if desired.

DID YOU KNOW?

Actor Gabby Hayes frequently shared the screen with John Wayne in the 1930s and '40s. In 1934 alone, the two starred in eight B-Westerns, including *The Lucky Texan*, *Blue Steel* and *The Star Packer*.

John Wayne, Ella Raines and Gabby Hayes in *Tall in the Saddle* (1944).

SOUTH-OF-THE-BORDER MEXICAN RICE

The perfect pairing with just about anything, this side dish works particularly well with spicier Latin cuisine.

PROVISIONS

- 2 Tbsp. olive oil
- ½ cup finely chopped onions
- 1 cup risotto rice
- 1 (15-oz.) can chopped tomatoes
- ½ tsp. ground cumin
- 1 clove garlic
- 1 jalapeño pepper, finely chopped (optional)
- 1 cup chicken stock

PREP

1. Heat a large skillet over medium-high. Add olive oil and chopped onions. Cook until onions are soft but not browned, about 3 minutes. Add the rice and cook, stirring, for 2 more minutes until the rice starts to look translucent. Put onion/rice mixture into a microwave-safe casserole dish with a lid. Put chopped tomatoes with their juice, ground cumin, garlic and jalapeño (if using) into a blender and blend until smooth. Add enough chicken stock to make 3 cups of liquid and blend.

2. Add the tomato/chicken stock mixture to the rice, stir, cover with the lid, and microwave on high for about 18 to 20 minutes. Stir 3 times while cooking. Remove from microwave, stir, replace lid and let stand 5 minutes. If not using the microwave, then add the tomato/chicken stock mixture to the rice in the skillet in 1-cup increments, stirring after each addition of liquid until fully absorbed.

DID YOU KNOW?

John Wayne knew the importance of enjoying a good meal. Once asked by *Variety* how he avoided overeating at lunch, he responded "I don't avoid overeating at lunch."

John Wayne in
Rio Grande
(1950).

ROASTED POTATOES

The old trail hands didn't have time to slave over fussy, elaborate recipes. Fortunately, as this standout side dish proves, that doesn't mean they skimped on flavor.

PROVISIONS

- 3 lb. baby Yukon gold potatoes
- 6 slices thick-cut bacon
- Olive oil
- ½ tsp. kosher salt
- ½ tsp. pepper
- ½ cup fresh Italian parsley, chopped

PREP

1. Preheat oven to 350 degrees F. Scrub potatoes and place in a large saucepan covered with salted water. Bring to a boil and cook for 5 minutes. Drain.

2. Cut bacon into small pieces and fry over medium heat until the fat has rendered and the bacon bits are crispy. Drain the bacon on paper towels and reserve. Pour the bacon fat into a measuring cup and add enough olive oil to make ½ cup.

3. Place potatoes in a roasting pan, add the bacon fat mixture, salt and pepper and toss to coat. Bake for 1 hour or until the potatoes are fork tender, stirring once or twice while cooking. Toss potatoes with the reserved bacon bits and parsley and serve.

DID YOU KNOW?

Duke's children Antonia, Patrick, Melinda and Michael traveled to Ireland for the shooting of *The Quiet Man* (1952) and worked as extras in the film.

Maureen O'Hara and John Wayne in *The Quiet Man* (1952).

SIDES

Gabby Hayes and John Wayne in *In Old Oklahoma* (1943).

HEARTLAND CREAMED CORN

You don't have to wait until summer to enjoy this delicious, creamy side dish.

PROVISIONS

2 cups fresh or frozen white corn

1 (15-oz.) can corn niblets, liquid reserved

1 Tbsp. salted butter

1 Tbsp. cream cheese, softened

2 Tbsp. all-purpose flour

3 Tbsp. milk

¼ tsp. pepper

PREP

1. Use a 4-quart slow cooker. Pour the frozen corn and the niblets from the canned corn into your slow cooker. Retain the liquid from the canned corn.

2. In a small saucepan on the stovetop, melt the butter and cream cheese over low heat. Slowly add the flour. Whisk until the flour is fully incorporated and remove from heat. Stir in the milk, juice from the canned corn and pepper. Pour this mixture evenly over the top of the corn in the slow cooker. Stir to combine. Cover and cook on low for 4 to 6 hours or on high for about 3 hours.

A WISE MAN'S MEAL
From left: Mae Marsh, John Wayne, Ward Bond and Ben Johnson in *3 Godfathers* (1948). The film was shot in Death Valley under the working title *Christmas Eve at Mojave Tank*.

DUKE'S MACARONI AND CHEESE

Lose the elbow macaroni, pilgrim; corkscrew pasta catches more cheese than the standard noodle, making this side the genuine article when it comes to this potluck classic.

PROVISIONS

- 1 (8-oz.) package corkscrew pasta
- 4 Tbsp. butter
- 4 Tbsp. flour
- 1 cup milk
- 1 cup cream
- ½ tsp. salt
- ¼ tsp. pepper
- 2 cups cheddar cheese

PREP

1. Preheat oven to 400 degrees F.

2. Boil pasta in water-filled saucepan. Cook for 10 to 12 minutes or until *al dente*, stirring occasionally. Drain.

3. Melt butter in a different saucepan. Whisk in flour, salt and pepper until well blended. Add milk and cream gradually and stir constantly.

4. Bring to a boil and cook for 2 additional minutes, stirring constantly. Lower heat and cook for 10 minutes, continuing to stir. Simmer for 5 minutes, adding cheese gradually and stirring. Turn off flame.

5. Add noodles to pan and stir into mixture. Transfer to a buttered baking dish and bake for 20 minutes or until top is golden brown.

Donna Reed and John Wayne in *Trouble Along the Way* (1953).

Common Bonds

In addition to being former USC football players, Duke and his Trouble Along the Way *co-star Tom Hennesy were also passionate about land development. The two became business partners in the Malibu area in the late 1950s.*

SIDES

273

John Wayne sits down for a meal with his children Michael, Antonia and Melinda.

SUPREME PASTA SALAD

John Wayne loved a hearty meal, and he didn't waste his time on delicate dishes. Forget lettuce salads and light vegetables. This recipe serves up veggies the way Duke would want them—in a recipe brawny enough to fill even a cowboy's stomach.

PROVISIONS

- 1 box tricolor rotini noodles
- 8 radishes, sliced
- 1 cucumber, quartered and sliced
- 1 yellow bell pepper
- 1-2 stalks celery, sliced
- ½ cup chopped broccoli
- ¼ cup chopped cauliflower
- 20 grape tomatoes
- 1 (6-oz.) can pitted black olives, sliced
- 16 oz. Italian salad dressing
- 2 oz. seasoned salt

PREP

1. Fill large pan with water, bring to a boil. Add pasta and cook for 9 minutes or until tender. Drain pasta. Rinse.

2. Slice vegetables. In large bowl, combine pasta, vegetables and olives. Add Italian dressing; toss until pasta, veggies and olives are well coated. Add seasoned salt; toss until veggies and pasta are well coated.

3. Cover and refrigerate for 4 hours before serving.

WAYNE FAMILY TIP

Nobody wants lukewarm food. To keep a cold side cool when serving outdoors, set your serving dish in a bigger bowl filled with ice.

SIDES

SCALLOPED CHEDDAR POTATOES

These rich, creamy potatoes are simple to make and go great with just about any dish. It's a stick-to-the-ribs side that won't disappoint.

PROVISIONS

- 3 lb. russet potatoes, peeled and thinly sliced
- 3 cups milk
- 1 clove garlic, minced
- 3 Tbsp. butter, softened
- 1 cup heavy cream
- 8 oz. cheddar cheese, grated
- Salt and pepper

PREP

1. Preheat oven to 325 degrees F. Combine potatoes and milk in a saucepan over high heat. Bring to a boil, then bring heat down to low. Cover and simmer for about 3 minutes or until potatoes are tender.

2. Drain potatoes and save the milk, making sure you have at least 2 cups.

3. Coat the inside of baking dish with garlic and butter. Add sliced potatoes and top with salt and pepper. Add saved milk and cream. Stir cheese into the potatoes.

4. Bake for about 85 minutes or until golden brown and milk has reduced and thickened.

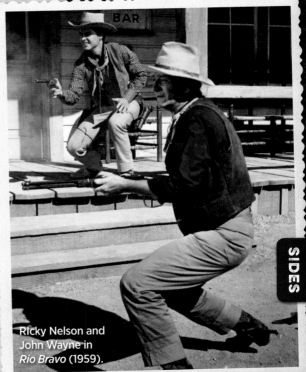

Ricky Nelson and John Wayne in *Rio Bravo* (1959).

SIDES

Duke and his youngest son, Ethan Wayne.

GRILLED GARDEN MEDLEY

This basic method for grilling eggplant, tomatoes and zucchini works for other vegetables too, including green onions and bell peppers.

PROVISIONS

- 2 **Tbsp. salt**
- 2 **medium eggplants, trimmed and sliced diagonally (about ¾ inch thick)**
- 2 **small zucchini, trimmed and halved lengthwise**
- 4 **Roma tomatoes, halved lengthwise**
- ⅓ **cup olive oil**

PREP

1. In a large bowl, dissolve 2 Tbsp. salt in 3 qts. cold water. Add eggplant slices and sink them with a small plate or bowl. Let sit for 30 minutes.

2. Meanwhile, prepare grill to medium-high heat.

3. Drain and dry eggplant. Lay vegetables on a platter. Brush one side with olive oil and sprinkle with salt.

4. Brush grill with vegetable oil. Lay vegetables on grill, oiled side down. Close lid of grill and cook until grill marks form, about 5 minutes.

5. Brush dry side of vegetables with olive oil and sprinkle with salt. Turn over, close lid of grill and cook until fork tender, about 3 to 5 minutes.

6. Serve while hot.

WAYNE FAMILY TIP

There are tons of ways to grill vegetables. Try wrapping zucchini, onions, sweet potatoes and all your other favorites in foil with some olive oil, salt and pepper, then put the whole thing on the grill.

SIDES

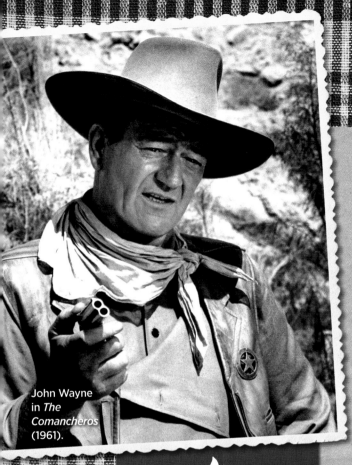

John Wayne in *The Comancheros* (1961).

BACKYARD COLESLAW

There's no better BBQ side dish than good old-fashioned coleslaw. Not only is it a classic that everyone loves, but eating this chilled salad on a sweltering afternoon will help keep you cool.

PROVISIONS

1   head cabbage, cored and shredded

4   large carrots, shredded

3   large celery stalks, shredded

1   cup mayonnaise

¾   cup sugar

PREP

1. After shredding vegetables, combine all ingredients in a bowl.

2. Refrigerate for 3 hours, stir and serve.

WAYNE FAMILY TIP

For a creamier, lighter slaw, substitute half of your mayonnaise with sour cream. It'll give the slaw a little zip and keep it from weighing you down.

ANGEL AND THE BADMAN BISCUITS

No matter how rough and tough your guests are, they're sure to have
a soft spot for these buttery biscuits.

PROVISIONS

- 5½ tsp. dry active yeast
- 4 Tbsp. sugar, divided
- ¼ cup warm water
- 2 cups milk
- 2 Tbsp. apple cider vinegar
- 5 cups all-purpose flour, plus more for rolling out the dough
- 1½ tsp. baking powder
- 1 tsp. baking soda
- 1 tsp. kosher or fine sea salt
- ½ cup vegetable shortening
- 4 Tbsp. melted butter

PREP

1. Combine yeast, 2 Tbsp. sugar and water in a small bowl. Whisk and let sit 5 minutes or until foamy.

2. Combine milk and apple cider vinegar and let sit for 5 minutes.

3. In a large bowl, whisk together the flour, baking powder, baking soda, 2 Tbsp. sugar and salt. Cut in the vegetable shortening until it resembles wet sand with some larger pieces of shortening. Add the yeast mixture and milk mixture. Stir to combine. Cover the bowl and let sit 1 hour. (Can also be stored in the refrigerator, covered, for up to 2 or 3 days—bring to room temperature before rolling out.)

4. Prepare the grill for indirect heat and preheat to high.

5. Flour a work surface and pat the dough out about 1½ inches thick. Cut out biscuits using a 2- to 3-in. round cookie cutter. Put biscuits in prepared skillets placing them close together. Brush the tops of the biscuits with more melted butter. Grill with the lid closed for 12 to 15 minutes or until the biscuits are golden brown, rotating the pan to keep the bottoms from burning.

6. Serve warm.

John Wayne and Gail Russell in *Angel and the Badman* (1947).

OLD-SCHOOL CREAMED SPINACH

You'll find creamed spinach on the menu at any great steak house, so why not pair it with the beef you grill at home? It'll become one of your dinner staples in no time.

PROVISIONS

- 4 bunches spinach (2½-lb. total)
- 2 Tbsp. butter
- ½ small onion, finely chopped
- 4 cloves garlic, finely chopped
- 1 (4-oz.) bar cream cheese, softened
- ½ cup milk
- Salt and pepper

PREP

1. Trim and wash your spinach.

2. Bring a pot of water to a boil. Add spinach and cook about 1 minute or until wilted. Drain spinach and rinse in cold water. Squeeze spinach, removing as much liquid as possible; chop and set aside.

3. In a saucepan, warm butter over medium heat. Add onion and garlic, seasoning them with salt and pepper. Cook for 3 to 4 minutes, stirring occasionally.

4. Add cream cheese and milk; stir until cream cheese is smoothly melted. Stir in spinach. Simmer over medium heat for 8 to 10 minutes or until it starts to thicken. Add salt and pepper to taste.

John Wayne poses for a publicity portrait during the early days of his Hollywood career.

SIDES

SWEET PEACH SALAD

Serve this salad when the sun's beating down and everyone's hunger is heating up.

PROVISIONS

- 3 ripe peaches
- Vegetable oil, for brushing
- 5 oz. washed baby spinach
- 4 green onions, sliced
- 2 tsp. sugar
- 3 slices thick cut bacon
- 1 Tbsp. red wine vinegar

PREP

1. Prepare the grill for direct heat and preheat to medium-high.

2. Cut the peaches in half and cut each half into 3 wedges. Brush the cut sides with oil. Grill 2 to 3 minutes per cut side or until nice grill marks are achieved but the peaches are still a little firm. Remove from grill and let cool.

3. Place the spinach in a salad bowl with the green onions and sprinkle the sugar all over.

4. Place the bacon in a cold skillet, turn the heat to medium and cook until very crisp, about 8 minutes, turning occasionally. Drain on paper towels and crumble. Add the vinegar to the skillet carefully (it will splatter) and cook until thickened, about 30 seconds. Pour the hot salad dressing over the spinach and toss to coat. Top with the grilled peaches and crumbled bacon. Serve immediately.

Maureen O'Hara and John Wayne in *Big Jake* (1971).

WAYNE FAMILY TIP

When shopping for peaches, you can test for ripeness by noticing a peach's color and firmness. Look for peaches that are dark yellow and have a little give when you grip them.

WAYNE FAMILY TIP

If you buy potatoes ahead of time, never store them in the refrigerator. Potatoes keep their texture best in a place that's dark and cool, not cold.

3 GODFATHERS GARLIC POTATOES

It would be a crime not to serve these delicious spuds at your next get-together.

PROVISIONS

- **2** lb. baby Yukon Gold potatoes (¾-inch diameter), washed and unpeeled
- **1** large white onion, cut in half widthwise and each half cut into 6 wedges
- **4** Tbsp. unsalted butter, cut into small pieces
- **3** garlic cloves, chopped
- **1** tsp. garlic powder
- **2** tsp. kosher or fine sea salt
- **1** tsp. freshly ground black pepper

PREP

1. Prepare the grill for direct heat and preheat to medium.

2. Place the potatoes in a cast-iron skillet in a single layer. Add the rest of the ingredients, stir well and cover the skillet snugly with foil. Put the pan over indirect heat and cover the grill. Cook for 30 minutes, remove foil, stir and cook uncovered for another 10 minutes or until the potatoes are tender.

3. To keep warm until serving, cover the pan with foil. The residual heat from the pan will keep the potatoes warm.

Mildred Natwick, John Wayne, Harry Carey Jr. and Pedro Amendáriz in *3 Godfathers* (1948).

SIDES

GENERATIONS OF GREATNESS
Robert Carradine and John Wayne in *The Cowboys* (1972). Carradine's father John Carradine starred with Duke in the legend's breakthrough film, *Stagecoach* (1939).

GREEN BERET GREEN BEANS AND BACON

Your family will be standing at attention once they get a bite of this hearty side.

PROVISIONS

- 1 lb. green beans, trimmed
- 3 Tbsp. olive oil
- 1 Tbsp. red wine vinegar
- 1½ tsp. Dijon mustard
- 4 slices bacon, cooked and crumbled
- ½ pint cherry tomatoes, halved
- Kosher or fine sea salt, to taste
- Pepper, to taste

PREP

1. Bring a large pot of salted water to a boil. Prepare a large bowl filled with ice water. Drop the beans into the boiling water and cook until crisp tender, about 4 minutes. Remove the beans from the boiling water and place directly in the ice water. Let cool at least 5 minutes. Drain well.

2. In a salad bowl, whisk together the oil, vinegar and mustard. Add the drained beans, bacon and tomatoes. Toss to coat. Add salt and pepper to taste.

Duke and his sons Patrick and Michael on the set of *The Green Berets* (1968).

DID YOU KNOW?

Duke's character in *The Green Berets*, Col. Mike Kirby, is based on a real World War II Finnish army captain named Lauri Törni, who later went by the name Larry Thorne.

NEW FRONTIER VEGETABLE SALAD

This simple, satisfying salad can take your barbecue to new territories.

PROVISIONS

- 3 red or yellow peppers, or a combination
- ¾ cup olive oil
- ⅓ cup balsamic vinegar
- 2 tsp. dried oregano
- 1 tsp. kosher or fine sea salt
- ½ tsp. pepper
- 1 large or 2 small eggplants
- 1 large white onion, cut into ½-in. slices
- 4 cups arugula
- 4 slices bacon, cooked and crumbled

PREP

1. Prepare grill for direct heat and preheat to medium-high.

2. Place the peppers on the grill whole and grill with the lid closed until the skin is blackened all over, turning occasionally, about 6 minutes. Remove from the grill, place in a bowl and cover with plastic wrap. Let cool at room temperature.

3. Whisk together the olive oil, vinegar, oregano, salt and pepper.

4. Slice the eggplant into ¼-in. thick slices and brush both sides with the oil and vinegar mixture. Brush the onion slices with the oil and vinegar mixture. Grill with the lid close until slightly charred and beginning to soften, about 4 to 5 minutes per side. Remove from the grill and brush again with the oil and vinegar mixture. Let cool.

5. When the peppers are cool enough to handle, scrape off the skins, cut in half and pull out the seeds and veins. Cut into ¼-in. thick strips and brush with the oil and vinegar mixture.

6. Toss the arugula with 3 Tbsp. of the oil and vinegar mixture. Place the arugula on a platter, top with the grilled vegetables and scatter the bacon over the top.

Helen Parrish, David Rollins, John Wayne and Marguerite Churchill in *The Big Trail* (1930).

WAYNE FAMILY TIP

After you finish cooking the bacon, reserve some of the extra fat and store it in the refrigerator for future use when you want to add some savory flavor to dressings and vegetables.

STAR PACKER POTATO SALAD

You'll never need to face off against a hungry crowd with this recipe up your sleeve.

PROVISIONS

- 3 lb. Yukon gold potatoes, peeled and cut into 1-in. pieces
- 2 Tbsp. plus 1 tsp. kosher or fine sea salt, divided
- 2 Tbsp. olive oil
- 1 Tbsp. white wine vinegar
- ½ tsp. pepper
- ⅓ cup mayonnaise
- ⅓ cup sour cream
- 6 green onions, thinly sliced
- 3 celery ribs, diced
- 1 tbsp. minced chives

PREP

1. Place the potatoes in a large pan and fill with cold water. Add 2 Tbsp. salt and bring to a boil. Reduce heat and simmer until the potatoes are tender, about 15 minutes. Drain and return the potatoes to the hot pot. Add the olive oil, vinegar, 1 tsp. salt, pepper and stir to coat the potatoes well. Let sit at room temperature to cool.

2. Once the potatoes have cooled, transfer to a large mixing bowl. Add the mayonnaise, sour cream, green onions, celery and chives. Stir well. Taste and add more salt and pepper if needed. Cover and refrigerate until cold, at least 4 hours. Can be made 1 to 2 days ahead.

John Wayne in *The Star Packer* (1934).

DID YOU KNOW?

The Matlock ranch house that appears in John Wayne's 1934 film *The Star Packer* is also used in two more of Duke's films: 1934's *Blue Steel* and 1935's *The Desert Trail*.

ALL-AMERICAN APPLE PIE

PAGE 310

DESSERTS

After a long day's work, you and yours certainly
deserve these easy-as-pie sweet treats.

Campfire Cobbler

Buckin' Berry Cobbler

Chocolate Bread Pudding

Skillet Chocolate Chip Cookies

Pumpkin Pudding

All-American Apple Pie

Peanut Butter and Chocolate Fudge

CAMPFIRE COBBLER

This dessert is a perfect way to end an evening spent under the stars.

PROVISIONS

- 2 **cups biscuit mix**
- 1 **cup sugar, divided**
- 1½ **cups milk**
- 6 **Tbsp. butter**
- 2 **cups peach slices, fresh or frozen and thawed**
- 1 **cup pitted sweet cherries, fresh or frozen and thawed**

PREP

1. Prepare the grill for direct and indirect heat, preheated to medium (350 degrees F).

2. In a mixing bowl, combine the biscuit mix with ¾ cup sugar. Add the milk and stir to combine.

3. Place the butter in a 9-in. cast-iron skillet. Place on the grill and heat until the butter melts. Add the biscuit batter to the pan and smooth into an even layer. The butter will bubble over the edges of the batter. Scatter the peaches and cherries over the top of the batter, sprinkle with the remaining ¼ cup sugar, close the lid and cook for 10 minutes. After 10 minutes, move the skillet to the indirect heat side, close the lid and cook for another 20 minutes or until a toothpick inserted into the center comes out clean.

John Wayne in *A Lady Takes a Chance* (1943).

DID YOU KNOW?

While *A Lady Takes a Chance* was directed by William A. Seiter, it was originally going to be helmed by Henry Hathaway, who would direct Duke's Oscar-winning role in *True Grit* (1969).

DESSERTS

BUCKIN' BERRY COBBLER

Hang tight! This cobbler packs a powerful kick of flavor.

PROVISIONS

FILLING

- ½ cup sugar
- 2 Tbsp. cornstarch
- 8 cups mixed berries (if using strawberries, limit to 1½ cups and cut them in half)
- Juice and finely grated zest of 1 lemon

DOUGH

- 1½ cups flour
- 4 Tbsp. sugar, divided
- 1½ tsp. baking powder
- ½ tsp. baking soda
- ½ tsp. kosher or fine sea salt
- 6 Tbsp. cold butter, cut into small pieces
- ¾ cup buttermilk

PREP

1. Preheat oven to 375 degrees F.

2. Prepare the filling. Combine the sugar and cornstarch in a mixing bowl. Add the berries, lemon juice and zest, stir and let sit while preparing the dough.

3. For the dough, whisk together the flour, 3 Tbsp. sugar, baking powder, baking soda and salt. Add the butter and, using a pastry cutter or your fingers, work the butter into the flour until it resembles a coarse meal with some bigger pieces of butter. Add the buttermilk and stir until combined.

4. Pour the filling into a cast-iron skillet. Drop tablespoonfuls of the dough on top of the berries. Sprinkle the dough with 1 Tbsp. sugar. Bake for 40 to 50 minutes or until the dough is golden brown and the berries are bubbling. Let cool a little before serving.

John Wayne and Duke the Horse in *Ride Him, Cowboy* (1932).

CHOCOLATE BREAD PUDDING

Chocolate and bread come together in one delicious dessert.

PROVISIONS

- 1 Tbsp. butter, softened
- 6 large eggs
- 3 cups chocolate milk
- ½ cup brewed coffee, cooled
- ½ cup light brown sugar, lightly packed
- ¼ cup heavy cream
- 1 Tbsp. pure vanilla extract
- 4 Tbsp. unsweetened cocoa powder
- 1 loaf white sandwich bread, cut into 1-in. cubes
- 1 cup semi-sweet or bittersweet chocolate chips

PREP

1. Preheat oven to 325 degrees F. Grease a 12-in. cast-iron skillet with the butter.

2. Whisk the eggs in a large mixing bowl. Add the chocolate milk, coffee, brown sugar, cream and vanilla, and whisk well. Whisk in the cocoa powder. Add the bread, stir and let sit for 15 to 20 minutes, stirring occasionally. Pour the bread mixture into the prepared skillet, add the chocolate chips and stir to distribute the chips throughout. Bake for 1 hour or until the custard is set and the top browned.

DID YOU KNOW?

After the release of *The Shootist* in 1976, Duke decided to spread awareness about the disease he dubbed "The Big C" by filming PSAs for the American Cancer Society.

John Wayne in *The Shootist* (1976).

WAYNE FAMILY TIP

Why choose one—some bakers recommend using both semi-sweet and bittersweet chocolate chips in their cookie recipes!

SKILLET CHOCOLATE CHIP COOKIES

If you like chocolate chip cookies (and who doesn't?), then we've found the right dessert for you.

PROVISIONS

1½ cups flour

1½ tsp. baking powder

½ tsp. salt

12 Tbsp. butter, at room temperature

1 cup light brown sugar, lightly packed

½ cup sugar

2 large eggs, at room temperature

2 tsp. pure vanilla extract

1½ cups semi-sweet or bittersweet chocolate chips

PREP

1. Preheat oven to 325 degrees F.

2. Whisk together the flour, baking powder and salt in a medium mixing bowl.

3. Place the butter and sugars into the bowl of an electric mixer preferably fitted with a paddle attachment. Beat on medium-high speed until light and fluffy, about 3 minutes. Add the eggs, one at a time, beating well after each addition. Beat in the vanilla. Turn the mixture to low and add the flour mixture. Beat just until the dough starts to come together, add the chocolate chips and stir in well with a spatula, making sure you scrape the sides and bottoms of the bowl.

4. Divide the mixture into three 5-in. cast-iron skillets or one 9-in. skillet. Bake small skillets for 20 to 25 minutes, 30 to 35 minutes in a large skillet, or until golden and set.

John Wayne in *True Grit* (1969).

PUMPKIN PUDDING

This creative concoction gives you the tasty filling of pumpkin pie without the hassle of making the crust.

PROVISIONS

- 1 (15-oz.) can pure pumpkin puree
- 1 (12-oz.) can evaporated milk
- ¾ cup white sugar
- ½ cup biscuit mix
- 2 large eggs
- 2 Tbsp. butter, melted
- 2 tsp. vanilla extract
- 1¼ tsp. ground cinnamon
- ½ tsp. nutmeg
- ¼ tsp. ground cloves
- ⅛ tsp. ground ginger

PREP

1. Use a 4-quart slow cooker sprayed with cooking spray. In a mixing bowl, combine all of the ingredients and whisk until fully blended. Pour the batter into the prepared insert. Cover and cook on high for 3 to 4 hours or on low for about 6 hours. Check your "pie" after 2 hours on high and 3 hours on low. Then check every 30 minutes.

2. When fully cooked, the pudding will look just like a finished pumpkin pie. The batter will have browned and will crack in a few places. The center will have set enough for you to touch it without getting batter on your finger.

3. Let it sit in the slow cooker with the lid off until room temperature. Then spoon it into serving dishes and top with whipped cream or serve with vanilla ice cream.

DID YOU KNOW?

Duke didn't just work in front of the camera. In addition to directing, he started producing films in 1947. The first film he produced was *Angel and the Badman*.

John Wayne in *El Dorado* (1967).

ALL-AMERICAN APPLE PIE

A classic recipe enjoyed by Americans for generations, this pie
makes a patriotic (and tasty) cap to any meal.

PROVISIONS

- 2 cups graham-style crumbs, divided
- 4 Tbsp. unsalted butter, melted
- 1 Tbsp. honey
- 4 large apples, peeled, cored and thinly sliced
- ¾ cup brown sugar, divided
- ½ lemon, juiced
- 1 Tbsp. cornstarch
- 1 tsp. ground cinnamon
- ¼ tsp. kosher salt
- 1 tsp. pure vanilla extract
- ½ cup sliced almonds
- 4 Tbsp. unsalted butter, softened

PREP

1. Line a flat baking sheet with foil and place on the lowest rack of the oven (this is to catch any juices that may drip from your pie and keep your oven clean). Put the other rack in the middle. Preheat oven to 350 degrees F. Spray a 9-inch pie pan with nonstick cooking spray.

2. Combine 1 ¼ cups graham-style crumbs with the melted butter and honey. Dump the mixture into the prepared pie plate and press firmly on the bottom and up the sides of the pan. Bake for 10 minutes. Leave the oven on.

3. In a large mixing bowl, combine the sliced apples, ½ cup brown sugar, lemon juice, cornstarch, cinnamon, salt and vanilla and toss to combine. Pour the mixture into the pre-baked pie crust and gently press down on the apples to flatten the top slightly.

4. Combine the remaining ¼ cup brown sugar with the remaining ¾ cup graham-style crumbs and sliced almonds. Cut the butter into pieces, and with your fingers combine everything until it is clumpy. Spread the mixture over the apples and bake for 80 to 90 minutes or until the apple mixture is hot and bubbly and the crust is browned; after 45 minutes place a piece of foil over the top of the pie to keep it from browning too much.

5. Let cool and serve.

Duke at USC, c. 1925.

PEANUT BUTTER AND CHOCOLATE FUDGE

PB and chocolate are like Ward Bond and Duke—an always welcome combo.

PROVISIONS

- 5 Tbsp. unsalted butter, use divided
- 2 cups light brown sugar
- ½ cup plus 3 Tbsp. heavy cream, divided
- 1 Tbsp. pure vanilla extract
- 1 cup creamy peanut butter
- 1¾ cups powdered sugar
- 1 cup semisweet chocolate chips
- 3 Tbsp. corn syrup

PREP

1. Line an 8-inch square cake pan with parchment paper with a 2-inch overhang of paper on all sides.

2. Melt 4 Tbsp. butter in a medium saucepan over medium-high heat. Add the brown sugar, ½ cup cream and the vanilla. Bring to a boil. Let boil for 2 minutes, stirring constantly. Add the peanut butter and stir until smooth. Take off the heat and let cool for 5 minutes.

3. Put the peanut butter mixture in a mixer preferably fitted with a paddle attachment. Mix on medium-low speed and gradually add the powdered sugar. Mix until everything is incorporated and smooth. Put the mixture in the prepared pan and smooth the top with a spatula.

4. In a small saucepan, melt the remaining 1 Tbsp. butter with the chocolate chips and corn syrup. Add the remaining 3 Tbsp. of cream and mix until smooth. Pour over the top of the peanut butter fudge and refrigerate until firm, at least 2 hours.

5. Cut into small squares and serve.

WAYNE FAMILY TIP

To guarantee your fudge has the perfect consistency, use a thermometer to make sure you are cooking it between 237 to 239 degrees F.

John Wayne and Ward Bond in *The Long Voyage Home* (1940).

INDEX

Cotija, 258
cream, 268, 284
Gorgonzola, 189
Monterey Jack, 108, 132
mozzarella, 89, 129, 262
Parmesan, 99, 129, 135, 262
pepper jack, 232
string, 262
Swiss, 247
Cherries
dried, 87, 162
fresh or frozen, 301
Chicken, 82, 87, 119, 123, 126
breasts, 94, 99, 100, 102, 105, 106, 108, 112, 129, 132
drumsticks, 91
fryer, 125
ground, 238
No-Punches-Pulled, 89
thighs, 85, 93, 115, 116, 120, 135, 136
Chili, canned, 229
Chocolate
chips, 305, 307, 312
milk, 305
Chutney, Major Grey's, 63
Cocoa powder, 305
Coffee, 40, 305
Cola, 165
Coleslaw, 87
mix, 156, 196
Corn
fresh, 181, 258, 268
frozen, 159, 258, 268
niblets, 268
Cornmeal, 14, 119, 261
Cornstarch, 12, 17, 302, 311
Corn syrup, 312
Cranberries, 162
Cucumber, 219, 275

D

Dressing, Italian salad, 275

E

Eggplants, 279, 294
Eggs, 12, 14, 18, 20, 23, 26, 28, 33, 119, 120, 129, 184, 262, 305, 307, 308
Evaporated milk, 308

F

Fish (and seafood)
anchovy fillets, 208
cod, 196
halibut, 196, 201
salmon
fillets, 199, 215
wild Pacific, 210
scallops, sea, 202
shrimp, 213
swordfish steaks, 205
tilapia, 196
trout fillets, 208
white, 219

G

Garlic, 31, 39, 43, 48, 61, 64, 71, 75, 99, 102, 105, 108, 115, 116, 135, 147, 148, 160, 165, 174, 176, 179, 181, 184, 189, 190, 201, 208, 210, 213, 242, 255, 264, 277, 284, 289
bottled, 91
Ginger, 112, 176
Ginger ale, 172
Graham-style crumbs, 311
Green beans, 106, 255, 292
Grits, 135
Guacamole, 48

H

Ham
deli, 28, 247
spiral-cut, 172
Harissa paste, 190
Heavy cream, 20, 112, 273, 277, 305, 312
Herbs
basil, 129
chives, 20, 47, 79, 102, 257, 297
cilantro, 33, 43, 44, 71, 85, 89, 93, 94, 108, 112, 132, 136, 159, 160, 196, 201, 258
mint, 202, 219
parsley, 64, 85, 116, 174, 184, 208, 267
rosemary, 56, 71, 126, 135, 189, 210, 213
thyme, 120, 193
Honey, 43, 71, 82, 100, 135, 143, 170, 172, 174, 311
Horseradish, 115

J

Juice
lemon, 64, 91, 99, 102, 105, 172, 184, 190, 205, 208, 213, 302, 311
lime, 43, 44, 48, 61, 71, 93, 94, 108, 112, 136, 159, 160, 170, 172, 176, 181, 201, 219, 232
orange, 48, 71, 91, 172, 202
pineapple, 87

K

Kale, 167
Ketchup, 61, 63, 82, 87, 165, 176, 223, 225, 251

marinara, 129
pizza, 262
red enchilada, 132
soy, 39, 91, 170, 176, 199
Sriracha, 170, 240
steak, 63
sweet chili, 225
tahini, 105
tamari, 170
Worcestershire, 28, 39, 61, 63, 66, 79, 82, 87, 112, 165, 225, 247
Sauerkraut, 148
Sausages
  bratwurst links, 148
  breakfast, 18, 242
  Italian, 147, 167, 242
Sesame seeds, 199
Shallot, 106
Sherry, dry, 91
Sour cream, 37, 48, 108, 196, 297
Spices
  cayenne pepper, 37, 59, 66, 69, 94, 151, 201
  chili powder, 40, 94, 159, 165, 205
  chipotle pepper (powder), 33, 87, 100, 112, 136
  cinnamon, 26, 172, 184, 205, 308, 311
  cloves, ground, 172, 308
  coriander, 61, 105, 184
  crushed red pepper (red pepper flakes), 61, 64, 85, 116
  cumin, 33, 43, 48, 61, 71, 93, 94, 105, 115, 132, 159, 160, 179, 181, 184, 205, 219, 264

garlic powder, 18, 37, 59, 61, 69, 82, 87, 94, 99, 100, 102, 119, 120, 125, 129, 140, 151, 159, 162, 165, 205, 234, 247, 289
ginger, 170, 172, 205, 234, 308
jerk seasoning, 176, 205
Italian seasoning, 129, 147
lemon pepper, 59
mustard, dry, 28, 61, 151, 251
nutmeg, 184, 308
onion powder, 18, 82, 87, 91, 94, 100, 102, 115, 125, 151, 165
oregano, 48, 85, 115, 116, 160, 294
paprika, 61, 105, 115, 119, 120, 125, 140, 145, 151, 165, 179, 215
  smoked, 37, 50, 69, 100, 160
parsley, 59, 247
sage, 234
thyme, 59, 115, 215
Spinach, 18, 135, 284, 286
Squash, summer, 105
Sweet potatoes, 18

T
Tequila, 112
Tomato(es), 79, 108, 159, 202, 223, 225, 238, 247
  canned, chopped, 264
  cherry, 77, 99, 102, 106, 255, 292
  diced with chilies, canned, 132, 232, 258
  fire roasted, canned, 33
  grape, 219, 255, 275

paste, 33
pear, 77
plum, 44, 136, 201
Roma, 279
tomatillos, 93, 160
Tortilla(s), 33, 44, 48, 108, 160, 181, 196
  chips, 132, 153
Turkey, ground, 240

V
Vanilla extract, 14, 26, 305, 307, 308, 311, 312
Vinegar
  apple cider, 82, 156, 165, 234, 251, 283
  balsamic, 77, 91, 116, 162, 167, 189, 210, 255, 294
  cider, 61, 182, 201
  red wine, 39, 79, 106, 174, 286, 292
  rice wine, 199
  sherry, 106, 116
  white wine, 66, 85, 115, 297

W
Whiskey, 66
Wine, white, 193

Y
Yeast, 283
Yogurt
  Greek, 105
  plain whole-milk, 184, 205

Z
Zucchini, 105, 279

CONVERSION GUIDE

IF YOU'RE COOKING WITH THE METRIC SYSTEM, USE THIS HANDY CHART TO CONVERT CUPS AND OUNCES TO LITERS AND GRAMS.

VOLUME	
¼ tsp.	1.25 mL
½ tsp.	2.50 mL
1 tsp.	5 mL
1 tbsp.	15 mL
¼ cup	60 mL
⅓ cup	80 mL
½ cup	120 mL
⅔ cup	160 mL
¾ cup	180 mL
1 cup	240 mL
1 quart	1 liter
1½ quarts	1.5 liters
2 quarts	2 liters
2½ quarts	2.5 liters
3 quarts	3 liters
4 quarts	4 liters

TEMPERATURE	
32° F	0° C
212° F	100° C
250° F	120° C
275° F	140° C
300° F	150° C
325° F	160° C
350° F	180° C
375° F	190° C
400° F	200° C
425° F	220° C
450° F	230° C
475° F	240° C
500° F	260° C

WEIGHT	
1 oz.	30 g
2 oz.	55 g
3 oz.	85 g
4 oz / ¼ lb.	115 g
8 oz / ½ lb.	225 g
16 oz / 1 lb.	455 g
2 lb.	910 g

LENGTH	
⅛ in.	3 mm
¼ in.	6 mm
½ in.	13 mm
¾ in.	19 mm
1 in.	2.5 cm
2 in.	5 cm

All recipe content and photography reprinted with permission from The John Wayne Family Cookbook, The John Wayne Way To Grill, The John Wayne Way to Barbecue and The John Wayne Cast Iron Official Cookbook published by Media Lab Books.

Cover, steak: Melanie Acevedo/Photolibrary/Getty Images; 2 John R. Hamilton/John Wayne Enterprises; 4 Album/Alamy; 8 David Smart/Stocksy; 18 Ronald Grant Archive /Alamy; 20 Photo 12/Alamy; 24 John Dominis/The LIFE Picture Collection via Getty Images; 26 TCD/Prod.DB/Alamy ; 33 Pictorial Press Ltd/Alamy; 39 Moviestore Collection Ltd/Alamy; 53 TCD/Prod.DB/Alamy ; 54 Shutterstock; 66 Everett Collection; 72 Album/Alamy; 82 Everett Collection; 89 AF Archive/Alamy; 99 Collection Christophel/Alamy; 110 Sunset Boulevard/Corbis via Getty Images; 113 Everett Collection; 119 TCD/Prod.DB/Alamy; 126 Photo 12/Alamy; 130 Stanley Bielecki Movie Collection/Getty Images; 140 Moviestore Collection Ltd/Alamy; 143 Album/Alamy; 145 Everett Collection; 147 colaimages/Alamy ; 148 SilverScreen/Alamy; 153 ZUMAPress/Alamy; 159 TCD/Prod.DB/Alamy; 160 Moviestore Collection Ltd/Alamy; 164 AF Archive/Alamy; 165 Lauri Patterson/iStock; 168 AP/Shutterstock; 179 AF Archive/Alamy; 181 John R. Hamilton/John Wayne Enterprises; 186 Paramount/Getty Images; 190 Everett Collection; 216 RKO/Kobal/Shutterstock; 223 Album/Alamy; 229 Photo 12/Alamy; 231 Photo 12/Alamy; 236 Denis Cameron/Shutterstock; 239 Ronald Grant Archive/Alamy; 240 Album/Alamy; 244 Kobal/Shutterstock; 251 Photo 12/Alamy; 252 PictureLux/The Hollywood Archive/Alamy; 255 Album/Alamy; 264 Album/Alamy; 270 MGM/Kobal/Shutterstock; 273 Ronald Grant Archive/Alamy; 280 PictureLux/The Hollywood Archive/Alamy; 283 Pictorial Press Ltd/Alamy; 286 United Archives GmbH/Alamy; 289 Photo 12/Alamy; 290 Warner Bros/Kobal/Shutterstock; 292 AF Archive/Alamy; 297 Moviestore Collection Ltd/Alamy; 301 Everett Collection; 302 Everett Collection; 318 Everett Collection; Shutterstock: 5 (3), 6, 222

Media Lab Books
For inquiries, call 646-838-6637

Copyright 2020 Topix Media Lab

Published by Topix Media Lab
14 Wall Street, Suite 4B
New York, NY 10005

Printed in Korea

ISBN13: 978-1-948174-49-7
ISBN10: 1-948174-49-9

CEO Tony Romando

Vice President & Publisher Phil Sexton
Senior Vice President of Sales & New Markets Tom Mifsud
Vice President of Retail Sales & Logistics Linda Greenblatt
Director of Finance Vandana Patel
Manufacturing Director Nancy Puskuldjian
Financial Analyst Matthew Quinn
Brand Marketing & Promotions Assistant Emily McBride

Editor-in-Chief Jeff Ashworth
Creative Director Steven Charny
Photo Director Dave Weiss
Managing Editor Courtney Kerrigan
Senior Editor Tim Baker

Content Editor Trevor Courneen
Art Director Susan Dazzo
Assistant Editor Juliana Sharaf
Designer Kelsey Payne
Copy Editor & Fact Checker Tara Sherman

Co-Founders Bob Lee, Tony Romando

JOHN WAYNE
ENTERPRISES

Topix Media Lab would like to thank John Wayne Enterprises, custodian of the John Wayne Archives,
for providing unfettered access to their private and personal collection.

Best efforts were made by Topix Media Lab to find and credit the photographers. Topix Media Lab makes no specific claim
of ownership of images contained in this publication and is claiming no specific copyright to images used.

The mission of the John Wayne Cancer Foundation is to bring courage, strength and grit to the fight against cancer.
www.johnwayne.org

Indexing by R studio T, NYC

TM20-01

Best Wishes
John Wayne